40 LESSONS TO GET CHILDREN THINKING

Philosophical thought adventures across the curriculum

PETER WORLEY

B L O O M S B U R Y

LONDON · OXFORD · NEW YORK · NEW DELHI · SYDNEY

Bloomsbury Education
An imprint of Bloomsbury Publishing Plc

50 Bedford Square
London
WC1B 3DP
UK

1385 Broadway
New York
NY 10018
USA

www.bloomsbury.com

First published in Great Britain 2015

A catalogue record for this book is available from the British Library.
A catalog record for this book is available from the Library of Congress.

ISBN:
PB: 9781472916082
ePDF: 9781472916105

10 9 8 7 6 5

Typeset by Geoff Ward, Tower Designs UK Ltd
Printed by CPI Group (UK) Ltd, Croydon, CR0 4YY

This book is produced using paper that is made from wood grown in managed, sustainable forests.
It is natural, renewable and recyclable. The logging and manufacturing processes conform to the
environmental regulations of the country of origin.

To find out more about our authors and books visit www.bloomsbury.com.
Here you will find extracts, author interviews, details of forthcoming
events and the option to sign up for our newsletters.

For Peter: the boy who wanted to philosophise, though there was no tomorrow.

Acknowledgements

I would like to thank the following people for helping me bring this project together, either directly or indirectly:

Holly Gardner my editor at Bloomsbury, Stephen Campbell-Harris, Steve Hoggins, David Birch, Andrew Day, Andrew West, Miriam Cohen-Christofidis, Joseph Tyler, Jason Buckley, Chris Gill, Steve Williams, Robert Torrington, Emma and Kate. And a special thanks for the invaluable advice from my 'logic and critical thinking consultant' Jennifer Wright at King's College, London. Any remaining errors are mine.

Thanks to The Philosophy Foundation patron Terry Jones, Deborah Lyons and Holly Gilliam at Python (Monty) Pictures Ltd for permission to use The Bridge of Death Scene from Monty Python and The Holy Grail and for providing a link to the official version of the scene.

Many thanks to Professor Christopher Gill, whose lecture on Stoicism whose lecture informed Thought Adventure 7: The Glass of Water.

The poem 'The Dog that Meowed' is dedicated to Dora at Eliot Bank School, Year 3, 2012-13. Thanks also to David Birch for the enquiry plan on page 32, to Jason Buckley for 'Magnets' on page 162 and to Steven Campbell Harris, TPF specialist for the suggestion of 'True/False' on page 163.

Online resources accompany this book at **philosophy-foundation.org/resources/40**

Please type the URL into your web browser to download the resources mentioned throughout the book.

CONTENTS

FOREWORD

First of all, this book is easy to use. Pick it up, flick through, find a session that interests you, and use it. However, the attentive and more patient reader can get a lot more from this book. As well as having a reasonably extensive section introducing philosophy itself, I've also cross-referenced this book with all my other books; it therefore functions as a kind of 'heart', pumping blood around all the others while connecting them too, as a single body.

Once Upon an If is a book about stories and storytelling for thinking. In that book, I make a distinction between 'thinking with' and 'thinking about' stories. My previous books have been concerned with using stories to 'think with' or 'through' them; using a story to bring an audience to an encounter with a philosophical problem or dilemma. In this book, I have developed some ways to 'think about' stories, or to tackle the thorny issue of textual interpretation with young people. Apart from a miscellany of entirely new sessions for the classroom, how to think *about* stories is the original, new idea that this book offers.

A word that you'll come across a good deal in philosophy when broaching *interpretation* is 'hermeneutics'. At first, I was going to avoid this rather intimidating, scary-sounding word altogether; the kind of word that puts people off philosophy. Then I started to research it. Its origins lie with the Greek god Hermes, the messenger and herald of the gods, often coming down from Olympus to carry messages to people of the human world. Hermes is described as 'crafty and full of trickery'[1]; he was warned by Zeus not to tell lies, though Zeus recognised in him ingenuity, eloquence and persuasiveness. Hermes promised that he would never tell lies. 'But,' he said, 'I cannot promise always to tell the whole truth.'[2] He was even said to have helped the Three Fates in the creation of the alphabet, so the association he now has with interpretation is apt, to say the least. Hermes, therefore, joins Ariadne (*The If Machine* and *The Philosophy Shop*), Demodocus (*The If Odyssey*) and Sheherazade (*Once Upon an If*) as the emblematic figure of this book.

Following David Birch, in his book *Provocations: Philosophy For Secondary Schools*, I will occasionally use the expression 'hermeneutic question' and this means that the question is one that asks the children to say something about what they think a certain passage means; a necessary first step before being able to critically engage with an issue, which is usually the role of the 'task question' that follows it.

PaRDeS (see Appendix 2) is the new, general method for bringing children to interpret a text, which can be added to 'The Concept Box' from *Once Upon an If* (which is another method for interpreting texts), but there are also some other, standalone sessions that tackle interpretation in different ways, such as 'The never-ending letter' (interpreting prose), 'The ghost' (interpreting poetry), the *Hamlet* section of 'The glass of water' (interpreting Shakespeare) and 'Humpty Dumpty' (thinking about *meaning* itself in the manner of Lewis Carroll).

With this book I also want to show the important role philosophy can play within the curriculum: helping a teacher both *diagnose* and *assess* conceptual understanding within the class before, during and/or after a teaching module (see Appendix 5 for more on this). Given all the warnings we read in the literature about 'teaching to understand' over 'teaching to the test', it's no small need that philosophy is able to meet in the repertoire of any good, self-improving teacher. Incorporating good facilitation with good teaching should be a natural, complementary coupling, where eliciting from the student through enquiry paves the way for what it is the teacher needs to teach; conferring the right knowledge, the right information and the right facts for *that* child or *this* class, *when* they need to know it. Or when they ask.

Peter Worley, The Philosophy Foundation, September 2015

INTRODUCTION
FREQUENTLY ASKED QUESTIONS

What is philosophy?

This is a notoriously difficult question to answer, so I will answer it with this caveat: when I explain what philosophy is I will explain what *I mean by it* and by doing so I will provide a *framework* for the purposes of being able to say what I do in the classroom, and what this book – and my other books – hopes to achieve. In other words, what I say philosophy *is* is not the whole story but my account should provide you with something to work with, to understand, to aim for and possibly assess (see Appendix 3 for a list of intellectual virtues).

So, philosophy, done well, should be a rigorous, structured, sequential conversation (with others or oneself) that is both collaborative and oppositional, that attempts to explore, explain and justify the structure and content of our thoughts in response to perceived problems and puzzles about reality, knowledge, value and meaning.

Philosophy employs a method/process (more often than not ongoing) of reflection, reasoning and re-evaluation, by employing the appropriate intellectual virtues or excellences, in order to make good, though *provisional* judgments about what seems (metaphysically) true, (morally) right, and (logically) coherent. The aim is to improve our understanding (also understanding what we *don't* understand) of: the world, ourselves, our experiences and other people, by refining how we think about those things. The hope is that, by doing philosophy, we learn to think better, to act more wisely, and thereby help to improve the quality of all our lives.

At the heart of this is the philosophical *process* captured in my 'Four Rs of philosophy'. According to these philosophy is:

- **Responsive** – philosophers (children or adults) respond to a problem that they have recognised, for themselves, to be a problem: 'That's not fair! But it kind of is fair as well!' (See 'Key controversies' on page ix.)
- **Reflective** – philosophers are invited to contemplate the nature of concept X or Y: 'What is *fair*, exactly?'
- **Reasoned** – philosophers should be guided to reason about what it is they have reflected on to attempt to order their thoughts supported by reasons: 'Fair is when you … because …', 'Fair can't be … because …', 'Fair must be … because …'
- **Re-evaluative** – philosophers should be invited to critically engage with the reflections and reasons offered either by others or by themselves.

Remember: philosophy in the classroom is about *doing* philosophy, not learning about the subject of philosophy; in short, it is about *philosophising*. I have focused on the four Rs because they are at the heart of the process of philosophising.

Why do philosophy with children?

First of all, thinking, questioning, challenging assumptions, contemplating, conversing, and many other intellectual virtues honed by doing philosophy, are central to what it is to be an exemplary human being. In addition, children are capable of doing all of these things, so it stands to reason that they should be invited to practise mastering these competencies from an early age so that they become second nature by adulthood.

Children also experience philosophical problems in their daily lives. I characterise a philosophical problem as what happens when your experience of the world doesn't fit with your understanding of it. For instance, a child may understand *time* to be constant (clocks run at a steady speed) but experience time as fluctuating ('Time flies when you're having fun!') or another child may think of herself as a single, unchanging unity but experience herself changing, growing and maturing ('I am the same person and I'm not the same person!'). Among other things, the job of education is to provide the tools to help students tackle problems they are likely to encounter. If children encounter philosophical problems, as I argue they do, then it should fall to the education system they are in to provide them with the tools to begin to approach and tackle those problems.

How will philosophy help the children in my class?

Philosophy is centrally concerned with concepts (basic ideas and notions that lie behind our words and thoughts), and one contention of this book is that *conceptual understanding* lies at the heart of any child's ability to successfully navigate his or her way through new topics of learning in the school curriculum (for example, one has to have a grasp of relational concepts to understand how words like 'big', 'small' or 'longer' work). Philosophy allows the children to think about and explore the concepts that lie at the heart of many curriculum topics, giving teachers an opportunity to diagnose, observe and assess their class's understanding of the concepts involved in a particular teaching module, whether it be *dissolving*, *art appreciation*, *forces* or *sound* and so on. Research has found, among other things, that doing philosophy improves performance in maths and literacy (Gorard et al 2015), confidence, speaking and listening, improvement in IQ scores (Tricky and Topping 2007), and reduction in psychotic tendencies (Garcia et al 2005). See Appendix 3 for more details of Intellectual virtues.

What prior experience or knowledge of philosophy do I need?

You need no knowledge of the subject of philosophy to use this book (though I hope you will learn something about philosophy while using it), but you will need to develop your questioning skills to be able to use it successfully, and you can do that *while* using the book, as a *result* of using the book. To begin with, familiarise yourself with Appendix 1: Facilitating idea diversity, which will furnish you with most of the tools you'll need to become a better questioner. The 'Key facilitation tool' entries, peppered throughout the book, contextualise many of the facilitation tools and strategies within the lesson plans and the classroom. My other books (and their accompanying online supplements) have some of the questioning and facilitation strategies explained in more detail, so, though it is not necessary to buy the other books to make use of this one, reading and using them may also supplement your facilitation skills:

- *The If Machine*: 'Section 1: How to do philosophical enquiry in the classroom', pages 1-45
- *Once Upon an If*: 'Storythinking' pp. 56-82 (especially 'Child-centred questioning', pages 68-70)
- *The If Odyssey*: 'Logos: Teaching Strategies for Developing Reasoning' pages 13-21

See bibliography for more reading to help develop your facilitation skills.

HOW TO USE THIS BOOK

Each of the 40 lessons in this book uses the same format with the same features to make it easier for you to put each one into practice. The elements they include are explained below.

Thought Adventure

A well-facilitated Thought Adventure (a stimulus followed by properly structured questions and activities) provides the conditions for the children to be able to see a philosophical problem for themselves understood and experienced *as a problem* (see the *responsive* R on page vii). When children 'see' a problem, it will often be seen as controversial, and this creates a 'buzz' in the room, an irrepressible hum of conversation. When this happens, we call it – what The Philosophy Foundation (TPF) specialist Steve Hoggins has coined – 'the bite point': when the philosophical puzzle has really bitten.

'Do' and 'Say'

To help the teacher use the lesson plans without having to wade through and separate instruction text from guidance and 'read out' text, I have distinguished *for you* that which is to be read out to the class and that which is meant for the teacher to do. This should save on preparation time and make the book much more pick-up-and-usable, usually requiring that you only read a lesson plan through once throroughly before using. I have, on occasion, when demanded – and *only* when demanded – included some instructional text inside the 'Say' box. Where this is necessary it is enclosed in a [square bracket]. So, where you see text in a [square bracket] inside a 'Say' box, this is NOT meant to be read out, however, this should be self evident from the context.

Equipment and preparation needed

As you would with a cooking recipe, you should at the very least carefully read through the lesson plan you intend to use. In addition, you should prepare whatever is mentioned in the 'Equipment and preparation needed' box at the start of each Thought Adventure. You should not need to memorise the session, simply follow the 'Say' and 'Do' boxes. If you are a storyteller or would like to implement more storytelling in your teaching and would like to tell some of the stories as opposed to reading them from the page, then see *Once Upon an If*: 'Sheherezad's Handbook' (pages 20-55) for some useful guidance on improving your storytelling; a very powerful technique for engaging your class.

Key controversies

Philosophical problems can be characterised as what follows when one recognises a conceptual controversy in one of the following ways:

1) An apparent contradiction: 'X and not X' (For example, 'I am the same person and I am not the same person.')

2) A conflict or tension between experience and understanding (For example, 'I understand time to be constant but my experience is that it fluctuates depending on whether I am asleep or awake, for example.'), which leads to 1, an apparent contradiction: 'time is constant and time is not constant'.

You could express most – if not all – the key controversies in this book in the form of an apparent contradiction, '*in a way* a thought is somewhere and *in a way* a thought is nowhere,' (see Here's a thought page 4); '*in a way* opposites are different and *in a way* opposites are not different' (see Poles apart on page 15); '*in a way* I know lots and *in a way* I know nothing' (see Know cards page 8) and so on. So, *in a way*, philosophy is about unpacking the 'in a way's in these apparent contradictions, either in order to unmask the contradiction as an imposter or to relinquish a formerly held belief *because* it leads to a contradiction. I have expressed the controversies in each Thought Adventure in the form of some key questions designed to bring out the apparent contradiction for the teacher. A good part of your preparation for a session would be to see if you are able to express the controversy as an apparent contradiction: 'In a way X and in a way not X' as in my examples.

Possible misconception

Philosophy sessions are a great way to identify and address common misconceptions that children have in and around subjects and topics. For example, that 'for something not to exist' means 'not being able to see it' (a misconception that may well feed into how children fail to understand a curriculum topic such as *dissolving* or *evaporation*). But I'd like to offer two words of warning about diagnosing misconceptions. First of all, children do not always mean exactly what they say and they do not always say exactly what they mean (see a discussion of this in 'Humpty-Dumptying' on page 139) so, a misconception is not necessarily the same as a misuse of language, or referring term or when someone is mis-informed or un-informed. Your questioning should involve a great deal of eliciting (see 'Opening up' on page 53) in order to avoid *mis*interpreting children's words. Secondly, teachers can have misconceptions too, so, be on the look out for *your own* misconceptions, either of the issue or with regard to what the children are trying to say. The philosophy sessions are also good for you - the teacher - to improve your understanding of yourself, your pupils and the issues and topics the philosophy sessions should engage *you all* with.

I have included common possible misconceptions in those sessions where I have been able to identify their re-occurrence when running that particular session. However, I should underline that they are only *possible* misconceptions, there may also be others and they may not be shared by all.

Key concepts and vocabulary

I have tried to identify the key concepts behind each session so that you can use the session to help do three things:

1) to *observe* your class in action manipulating concepts
2) to *diagnose* the class's grasp of key, relevant concepts before being taught the relevant module
3) to *assess* the class's application of the key concepts once the module has been taught or during its being taught.

These sessions, therefore, can be used before, during and/or after a teaching module. For instance, if you are about to teach a module on *dissolving* then 'The incredible shrinking machine' (on page 101) could be run in order to see how the children approach thinking about the microcosm. Do they think that something that can't be seen still exists or not? Which children think what? Do those that recognise that 'not being able to see something doesn't mean that it doesn't exist' make a convincing case to the others? Who has relevant knowledge and vocabulary (atoms, evaporation etc.)? By keeping a record of the answers to these and similar questions the philosophy sessions can help you plan your teaching of the module and can help deal with such things as differentiation and peer-to-peer support in the class.

Key facilitation tool

I have tried to find a context for most of the Key facilitation tools that are described in this and my other books. Here, it tells you which facilitation tool will be of special importance in this particular session and the page reference will be given for where the full description can be found.

Extension activities

These are not necessary parts of the main session, but can be pulled upon for a variety of reasons. Either because something relevant to a particular extension activity came up during the discussion, or because the curriculum aims and objectives call for a particular focus, or just to keep the pace of the lesson up. For example, running an entire hour-long session on the question 'Is there a thought on this piece of paper?' (see 'Here's a thought' on page 4) for some classes would be trying, for others not. For those that struggle, the extension activity 'telepathy trick' is an excellent way to keep them interested and to do something a little different. The extension activities also make excellent, sometimes more advanced, related follow-up sessions to the main session. Where they are more advanced I've said so. In some cases, such as with 'The Hodja's first day teaching' on page 45, I've managed to squeeze more than one Thought Adventure into one session. There's value for money!

Question types

- **Start question:** on page 116 I make a distinction between a 'surface level question' and a 'deeper level question'. Start questions are surface level questions that have no philosophical value in and of themselves but that are necessary steps to get things started. Example: 'What's going to happen next?'

- **Task question:** this will be the main question around which a philosophical enquiry (PhiE) will revolve. When anchoring (see page 7) these will be the questions you anchor to in order to help develop the formulation of arguments in the children's thinking and expression. These should be asked explicitly and written up on the board. Example: 'Is there a thought in this question?'

- **Hermeneutic question:** this is a question to do with the interpretation of something. Before you can critically engage (Example: 'Do you agree with X?' or 'Do you think X is right?') with someone or something you sometimes need, first of all, to think about what might be meant by the question or text (Example: 'What do you think X means by…?'); in other words, it may need 'unpacking'.

- **Nested question:** these are the further, implicit questions that lie behind the more explicit *start*, *task* or *hermeneutic* question. For example, if I ask the task question, 'Is there a thought in this question?' then there are a series of further questions we must, at some point, consider, such as, 'What is a thought?', 'Where are thoughts?', 'What is a question?', 'How are thoughts and questions (or language) related?' and so on. Looking through – or constructing for yourself – a list of nested questions around an issue or task question is a good way to prepare your view of the 'conceptual landscape'; in other words, to prepare for what's involved, conceptually.

- **What is X?-questions:** (also known as Socratic questions) these are open, abstract, reflective questions that take you to the basic concepts involved in the issue or task question. In most cases, there should be at least one of these in your list of nested questions. Examples: 'What is thought?', 'What is time?', 'What is language?' and so on. When there's more than one, you also have to consider how these basic concepts are related to each other, for example: 'What is light?', 'What is dark?', 'How are they related?'

- **Emergent questions:** these are the questions that are not planned but which emerge from the group naturally and that can be used as task questions with a class. Sometimes someone in the class asks the question explicitly during a discussion, 'Can something be so, so, so, so small that it can't exist?' (8-year-old Alice). Or, someone may say something in the form of a statement that can be reformulated into a question and put to the class as a task question. For example, Alice may have said, 'Some things are so, so, so, so small that they can't exist.' The facilitator may then, legitimately say to the class, 'So, what do you all think about that? Can something be so, so, so, so, small that it can't exist?' The facilitator then writes the question up on the board and gives the class talk time following the procedure for an enquiry around a task question described on page iii. A facilitator should always be on the look out for good emergent questions.

PRACTICALITIES

How should I set the classroom up?

- *Space to think – the 'talk circle'*: Clear the tables away and arrange the chairs into a horseshoe shape so that the children can see each other's faces, the board (if necessary) and you. I call this the 'talk circle' and many practitioners of philosophy with children consistently find that this is the format most conducive to conversation-based lessons, as the participants can clearly see each other. It also provides space within the circle for props, drama, games and activities – what you might call 'space to think'.

- *A quick 'talk circle'*: You may want to incorporate a session plan into a lesson of your own, where it may be necessary for the pupils to stay at their desks to do writing or note-taking. Try to have a 'quick talk circle' procedure planned and rehearsed with your class: each student should have a place they go to with their chair (reasonably close to their normal place). If you say, 'Let's do the quick talk circle!' then they go to that place, probably at the edge of the classroom so they can more or less see each other. This can also work in classrooms where there just isn't space to move tables around.

- *The 'talk ball'*: I always have a soft – but not too bouncy – 'talk ball' with me. I find it an indispensable piece of kit for helping manage discussions, especially with large numbers of people, children or adults. 'The ball rule' (see below) is a helpfully visual way for the children to keep themselves in order throughout an enquiry. (See also 'How do I run an enquiry?' on page ii for more on this).

- *Rules*: These are my 'five rules of philosophy' that I establish clearly in the first session and quickly remind children of at the start of each session if necessary:

  - *The ball rule* – that one 'may only speak when holding the talk ball'.

  - *The listening rule* – that one 'does their best to listen to in order to understand whoever it is that has the ball'.

  - *The hands up/hands down rule* – 'hands up if you want to say something, but hands down again when someone has the ball and is talking or thinking.'

  - *The respect rule* – this captures all behaviour expectations, but it can be helpful to remind the class that they 'may still disagree with each other, as long as they do so respectfully'.

  - *The stop-look-listen rule* – 'when I hold the ball up in the air this means to stop talking, to look this way and be ready to start a discussion.'

How long should a session take?

I usually run sessions in schools for anywhere between 45 minutes to an hour, depending on age, maturity, and engagement. Having a time slot such as this put aside each week for philosophy where you use the lesson plans you'll find in this book is a good starting place for doing philosophy. The aim, however, is to incorporate your facilitation and questioning skills into your normal curriculum teaching. You may be doing something on 'the growth of trees' and, without any perceptible change, you suddenly allow the class to pursue a line of enquiry around the difference between *building* and *growing* for instance, you may make a few mental notes such as who knows what, how they understand *growth* and *building* to be related, who thinks they are the same, who thinks they're different and who that they're similar and so on. It was only five minutes of enquiry but it was just what you needed to see how to proceed with your teaching of the growth of trees. So, in the end, and in the hands of a good teacher, an enquiry is as long as it needs to be.

How do I run an enquiry?

Here's a quick answer:

1 Set up the talk circle (see page xii).
2 Establish or remind the class of the rules (see 'Rules' on page xii).
3 Present the stimulus (e.g. read or tell the story or poem, perform the trick and so on).
4 Ask the task-question (e.g. 'Is talking good?') or run the desired procedure (e.g. PaRDeS, Concept Box and so on).
5 If asking a task-question then clearly write it up on the board.
6 Allow a minute or two of talk time where they should all talk to each other in pairs or small groups.
7 Show the sign for the 'stop-look-listen-rule' (see 'Rules' on page xii).
8 Ask the task-question again.
9 Conduct your whole-class enquiry (See Appendix 1: 'Facilitating idea-diversity' and 'Key facilitation tools' in each session for specific facilitation tools and skills) around the session plan you have chosen.
10 Periodically, allow more talk times, then return to the whole-class enquiry (see step 9), introducing new questions when appropriate and/or returning to the main question when appropriate.
11 Run any extension activities as required, complete with whole-group enquiries (see step 9).
12 (Optional) Round off by asking meta-cognitive questions, such as:

'Has anyone come to any conclusions about the main question? Would you like to say anything about what you think now?'

'Did anyone change their mind during the discussion? Why?'

'Did anyone hear an idea they particularly liked? What was it and why?'

13 (Optional) It is advisable to finish with a game. There are plenty of games available for free for members of *The Philosophy Foundation* website: www.philosophy-foundation.org/members (it's free to become a member!) and there are some good games in Robert Fisher's book *Games For Thinking*.

Remember: this is <u>not</u> a PhiE (philosophical enquiry); this is the procedural structure in which you hope a PhiE will occur. The PhiE, one hopes, happens in steps 9 and 10 when, and if, the discussion is well-focused and well-facilitated. Look for the Four Rs happening (see 'What is philosophy?' on page vii). And that leads you to the long answer: good questioning and facilitation (see especially 'Appendix 1: Facilitating idea diversity' and 'Key facilitation skills' throughout this book for more on the long answer).

Community of enquiry

Most, if not all, of these Thought Adventures will also work with the well-known 'Community of Inquiry/Enquiry' (CoI) P4C procedure. The basic procedure, though there are many variations of this, is as follows:

1 The stimulus is presented (story read, object displayed etc.)
2 Think time is given.
3 Questions are formulated by the children in response to the stimulus.
4 Questions are gathered on the board and sorted into categories such as philosophical questions, factual questions etc. (see Philip Cam's 'Question Quadrant' in 20 Thinking Tools).
5 The relevant questions (after sorting) are put to a classroom vote.
6 The question that is voted for by the class is then used as the start of an enquiry.
7 The children enter into a facilitated discussion around the chosen question.

If using a Thought Adventure for a CoI then simply use the stimulus (story, poem, activity and so on) and then follow the procedure above (or whichever variation on this you wish to use) to conduct your CoI.

Age ranges

These sessions have been devised for UK Key Stage 2 (7-11-years-old) and most of the lesson plans will work with all these age ranges with a little adaptation in some cases; many will work with Key Stage 3 (12-years-old) and above with a little adaptation in some cases. Some sessions will work less well with younger children; they are listed here with suggested starting ages:

Know cards	9 years and up
Vouchers	10 years and up
The glass of water	10 years and up
If a rock tumbles…	9 years and up
The maybe cat	9 years and up
A plan	10 years and up
Who's right?	10 years and up
The hypothesis box	10 years and up
When worlds collide	10 years and up
Perspectacles	10 years and up

THE GHOST

Thinking about ghosts, time and poetry

Introduce the children to a ghost, sneak some poetry up on them and acquaint yourself with a method for approaching poetry.

Equipment and preparation needed

- An old-looking wooden box
- The two poems from the lesson written on to two pieces of paper, folded up and placed in the box (number them 1 and 2, so that you take them out in the right order)

Subject links

Literacy
Poetry
RE

Key controversies

What is a ghost? Do ghosts exist? Is a poem by a deceased poet the voice of a ghost?

Key concepts and vocabulary

Books
Communication
Death

Metaphor
Tense
Time

Possible misconception

Understanding metaphors literally

Key facilitation tool

Approaching poetry (see page 2)

Do: Begin by reading the following second-person scenario.

Say: One day you are told to help out in the garden, and you are given the job of digging the soil to turn it over. Not your favourite thing, but you kind of have to do it. During your digging, your spade hits something. You think it's just another rock, but it doesn't feel like the rocks your spade has already hit. You put your hand into the soil under your spade and feel around. Your fingers touch a pointed corner. There's something there that's no ordinary rock or root! So you take your spade and start to dig around the object, whatever it is. After a while you remove a box from the ground that looks very old. It must have been there for a long time, you think. The box is closed, so will you open it? You find that it opens easily. Do you look inside? You must decide. You do open it. Inside the box you find two pieces of old parchment, one with the number '1' written on it, and the other with the number '2'. They are yellowed with age and cracked at the edges. You take out the one labelled '1'. You have to be very careful with it, as it is so old it begins to crumble at your touch. However, you can just read what's written on it. It appears to be a poem. It says …

Lines written by someone now dead

You can't quite see me but you know I'm there
Can't hear me, but you could swear
That someone's talking, reaching out for you
Through the white of this paper, from out of the blue.

A ghost of words on a ghost-coloured page,
The ghost of the poet behind a black-and-white cage,
An echo of thought, once had, now dead
That shimmers through time when these words are read.

KEY FACILITATION TOOL

Approaching poetry

The following is a procedure adapted from *Thoughtings* (see Links) for approaching poetry with primary-age children (ages 7–11):

1. Read the poem.

2. Allow the children a few seconds of silence to 'take it in'.

3. Read the poem again, but leave out a few key words (usually rhyming ones, but not necessarily) for the class to fill in.

4. Project, or hand the poem out (usually one between two), and allow the children to respond in pairs. At this stage allow them to respond how they like, so no task question (see below).

5. Take responses in the talk-circle as a short enquiry. (Be on the look-out for good emergent enquiry opportunities from this stage. An 'emergent enquiry' is an unplanned enquiry that emerges naturally from the children's contributions.)

6. Ask children to put up their hands if there is a word or phrase that they don't understand for the group to tackle on their behalf.

(For example, someone might say 'I don't get the bit that says, "the ghost of the poet behind a black-and-white cage".')

7. Do a response detector (see Appendix 1) to make sure that the next contribution is connected to contributions made in Step 6.

8. If necessary, ask if there are any other words or phrases that are not understood, until all of the poem has been 'unpacked' as much as the class is able, or until a good enquiry emerges (this will depend on your own aims and objectives).

9. For this particular poem, if necessary, use one of the following questions: Who has written the poem? Are they talking to you? Is he/she a ghost? What colour are ghosts? What is the 'black-and-white cage'?

10. You may decide at some point to read the poem again, or have the children do so. One child could read it, or you could ask different children to read one line of the poem each.

Say: After reading the first piece of parchment, you reach in and take out the second – the one with the number '2' written on it. It reads:

> **To the finder of these lines**
> Now write your own lines
> And place them in the box
> Bury it underground
> Under soil and rocks.
>
> Perhaps, one day
> Your lines will be found
> So that your silent, buried words
> May sound.

TIME CAPSULE ACTIVITY

Do: Hand out a piece of blank paper to each child.

Say: Following the invitation by the mystery poet, write your own words to put into a box to be read by someone hundreds of years from now. You can write anything you want – it can be a poem, but it doesn't have to be. Whatever you decide to write, make sure that it's something you want someone to read hundreds of years from now when they dig it up from the ground.

Task question: **Can a poet live forever through his or her work?**

Nested questions

• What would 'living forever' be?   • Is 'live' used literally or figuratively in the task question above?

EXTENSION ACTIVITY

One-word Epitaph

Do: Project or hand out the following poem before reading it.

One-word Epitaph

Done? Gone?
Won? John.
Tripped? Slipped?
Lied. Tried?
What one word would you decide
To leave to say how you lived and died? _____.

Nested questions (the task question is in the poem)

• Can you sum up your entire life with just one word?

• What one word would you use to recommend to someone how to live?

• What values does your word signify?

• Can your life be put into words?

• If there were a book with every detail of your life described, would the whole of your life have been described?

• What do the words listed say about the person/each of the people who left them?

Links

Once Upon an If: pages 25–26; 28; 79–82

The If Machine: The Little Old Shop of Curiosities

The If Odyssey: The Concealer (The Island of Kalypso); Epilogue, page 155

The Philosophy Shop: Philosophical Poetry; Much Ado About Nothing; The Time Diet; The Pill of Life

Thoughtings: Love, Goodness and Happiness; Archaeology; Anthology of Unwritten Poems – for more on the Key facilitation tool: Approaching poetry

HERE'S A THOUGHT

Thinking about thought

Philosophy is sometimes said to be 'thinking about thinking'; in this session the children are invited to 'think about thoughts', and you get to perform telepathy to the class. This is one of those sessions where the children get to see the magic of the real world.

Equipment and preparation needed
- A piece of A4 paper to write on

Key controversies
Though it may be easy to locate the causes of a thought, where exactly is a thought itself?

Subject links
Literacy
Poetry

Possible misconception
That a thought is the same as the word 'thought'

Key concepts and vocabulary

Aboutness	Mind
Brain	Thought
Intention	Writing

Key facilitation tool
Provoke (see page 6)

Do: Write the following question on a piece of paper:

Is there a thought on this piece of paper?

Nested questions
- What is a thought?
- Where are thoughts?
- How are thoughts created?
- Where do thoughts that aren't being thought about go?
- Where are thoughts located?

AN EXERCISE IN TELEPATHY?

Do: Ask the class if they know what 'telepathy' is? Take ideas, then explain that it is 'when one transfers thoughts from one's own mind into the mind of another simply with the power of thought'.

Say: I will now transfer a thought from my mind into your minds without speaking.

> **Do:** After some theatrics – such as touching your forefingers to your temples – simply write: 'pink elephants' on the board. See the 'Provoke' Key facilitation technique on page 6.

Task question: ▸ **Did I just do telepathy?**

Nested questions

- What is telepathy?
- If this is not telepathy, then what would be?
- Did I transfer a thought?
- Is there a difference between transferring a thought and telepathy?

> **Do:** Invite the children to think about and respond to the following quote from Stephen King: 'What writing is. Telepathy, of course.'

Task question: ▸ **Is writing a kind of telepathy?**

If two people read the same words, do they have the same thought? For example, ask two friends to read this sentence:

The cat sat on the mat.

Do they both have the same thought?
What about:

…a green thought in a green shade. (Andrew Marvell)

- Has Andrew Marvell performed a kind of telepathy? (He has been dead for many years.)
- 'The reading of all good books is like a conversation with the finest minds of the past centuries.' – Rene Descartes. Discuss.

Links

The If Machine: Thinking About Nothing; The Ceebie Stories
The Philosophy Shop: Metaphysics; Philosophy of Mind
Thoughtings: Minds and Brains

Provoke

Do something that provokes a reaction. In the case of the Thought Adventure 2: Here's a thought (page 4): 'perform' telepathy. The question to anchor to when using this strategy for thinking is: 'Did I do X?' Immediately the children are invited to critically engage: 'No, because you just wrote it!' – then open up – 'So, why is that not telepathy?' and so on …

The main ways to engage a class in this way use the following:

- A question ('What is *now*?')
- A statement ('There's no such thing as *now*,' said eight-year-old Briony), usually drawn from the class
- A task ('Do something that changes the future!') – see 'Doing philosophy' on page 68 for more detail
- A performance ('I shall now change the future by spinning to the right instead of to the left like I said I would!'… 'Did I change the future?') – see 'An exercise in telepathy' on page 4.
- An experience (see 'The Never-Ending Letter' on page 98 for an example of how an experience can jolt participants into a response)

Anonymity: putting on the ring of Gyges

In *The If Machine* there is a chapter called 'The Ring of Gyges' in which the idea of a ring of invisibility is introduced. The ancient Greek philosopher Plato (c. 428–348 BCE) introduced this fantastical intervention to have his readers suppose that they could avoid being caught in order to have them consider whether there are any good reasons to act well, beyond the punitive. If you require sincere responses from the class, inviting them to respond from the perspective of invisibility (anonymously) can be much more effective than simply asking them to be sincere. This exercise is one that you can use in many other teaching and learning contexts from problem solving tasks to other ethical discussions. (See page 14 for examples of its application.) Also recommended for this session is the strategy of *is/ought questioning* (see page 71).

Links

Provoke: See 'Art detectives' on page 145 for more on this general method of engaging a class.

Anchoring

This is the technique of asking a simple but central (usually grammatically closed) question that you keep coming back to.

In the case of Thought Adventure 3: Know cards (page 8), the question is 'Did X know where the black card was?', or 'Does X know where the black card is?' Keep coming back to these or similar questions over and over again, but always remember to 'open it up' if necessary (see Appendix 1). Anchoring helps to do the following:

• Keep the discussion focused

• Keep contributions relevant

• Reveal hidden relevance

• Link ideas to the task question

• Avoid dismissive comments from the teacher

• Avoid premature judgement on the part of the teacher

• Avoid unnecessary confrontation

• Prompt children to contribute/remind children of question

• Formulate and express formal arguments

• Avoid over-complex language in the teacher's questions

KNOW CARDS

Thinking about knowledge

'How do you know that?' is one question, but philosophers ask, 'How do you know that you know that?' This session is designed to start a class on the task of producing an account of what it is to know something, and for you to have some fun with cards.

Equipment and preparation needed
- A deck of playing cards
- A readiness to improvise

Key controversies
Can one know something 100% for certain? Is it possible to provide an account of the conditions needed for knowledge? Do we know what will happen in the future because of what has happened in the past? What is knowledge?

Possible misconception
That 'being sure' is the same as 'knowing'

Subject links
Science
All other knowledge-based subjects

Key facilitation tool
Anchoring (see page 7)

Key concepts and vocabulary
Believing   Justification   Scepticism
Certainty   Knowledge   Seeing
Doubt

Do: Place two cards face down on the floor in the middle of the talk-circle. One should be a red card (any red card) and one should be a black card (any black card). Make sure no one sees them, and make sure that you know which is which. Put a small piece of paper next to each – one with 'A' written on it and the other with 'B' written on it. Leave these where they are for the duration of the session, as they will help when anyone wants to refer to the cards.

Say: I need a volunteer to point to the card that they think, out of these two cards, is the black card.

Do: When the volunteer (player) has pointed, record their suggestion on the board (continue to record players' suggestions and the actual positions of the cards as necessary):

First player's suggestion: (A) Red   (B) Black

Make sure the class know how to read what's on the board. Then, reveal which card is which. If the player selected the correct card, move on to the task question. If the player did not, keep playing until someone selects the correct card. Now move to the task question.

Nested questions

- What is it to know something?
- What does someone need to do to be able to say that they know something?

At this point you need to be ready to do whatever is needed to 'test' what the children say. After each of the 'tests', both before and after revealing which card is which, anchor them to the task question: 'Did/Does the player know where the black card was/is?'

Likely scenarios

1. If student says: 'No, because it was 50/50.' (Or words to that effect.)

Say: Let's test it. (I usually say this before each and every 'test' that I do.)

Do: Pick up the cards and then shuffle them, but make sure that you have two black cards this time. Play the game again. When it is revealed that the cards are both black …

Say: The player was unable to get the card wrong; whichever card they chose they would have been right. So, does that mean that they knew where the black card was?

Task question: Did the player know where the black card was?

2. If student says: 'No, because they couldn't see the cards.'

Do: Pick up cards and *show* the cards that you will put down. Make sure that you do something to throw doubt on the cards you've shown being the cards on the floor, by walking behind the board or doing something 'fishy' with your hands. Do not, however, change the cards from the ones you showed the children. Place them down as you showed them. Then play the game again, revealing which card was which.

Say: You saw the cards, and the cards <u>are</u> as you saw them. So, did X know where the black card was?

3. If student says: 'No, because you may have been lying to us.'

> **Do:** Pick up the cards and show the children the cards that you will put down. Do something 'fishy' again. Place them down as you showed them.

> **Say:** I showed you them, I have put them down as I showed you, and I am not lying to you. So, do you know where the black card is?

4. If student says: 'No, because we don't know whether you're telling the truth or not.'

> **Do:** Reveal which card is which, then …

> **Say:** There! I <u>was</u> telling the truth. Does that mean that, before I turned the cards over, you knew where the black card was?

If the children have noticed that you have used the same cards every time (except for the two black cards example) then ask the following two questions, though not at the same time:

> **Say:** X [name] has noticed that I have used the same cards every time. Does that mean that all the players so far knew where the black card was? Does it mean that the next player will know where the black card is?

> **Do:** Carry on in this way, testing each of their claims about why X didn't know, but always try to leave room for doubt in whatever it is you do. Always try to leave room for doubt until you come to the climax of the session. At some point …

> **Say:** OK, many of you have said [only say this if it's true] that you can only know something if you see it for yourself.

> **Do:** Place the cards down again, face up so everyone can see – then, in clear view of everyone and with no trickery or 'fishy' behaviour, turn the cards face down again.

Task question: Do you know where the black card is?

THE FINAL FLOURISH

For the very last situation …

Do: Again in plain view, turn the cards over (face down), asking for a show of hands of those that:

a. Think they know, then

　　Think they know 100% for certain

　　Think they know, but not 100% for certain

b. Think they don't know

c. Just don't know

Then, turn the cards over (face up) so that the entire class can plainly see them.

Say: Do you know now where the black card is? [Again, ask for a show of hands of those that]:

a. Think they know, then

　　Think they know 100% for certain

　　Think they know, but not 100% for certain

b. Think they don't know

c. Just don't know

EXTENSION ACTIVITY

Ask the class to come up with examples of things they know 100% for certain. For each example, ask the rest of the class whether they agree or disagree with the example given.

Task question: **Is example X an example of something you know 100% for certain? Why or why not?**

Links

Once Upon an If: The Six Wise Men; Flat Earth; Honest Sa'id; The Fire Stick; Sindbad and The Island

Philosophy for Young Children: Chapter 7: Epistemology: Dreams and illusions

Plato Was Wrong! Chapter 3: What do I know?

The If Machine: The Robbery

The If Odyssey: The Concealer; The Storyteller; The Stranger

The Philosophy Shop: Epistemology: Knowledge

Thoughtings: How do you know that?

VOUCHERS

Thinking about the distribution of wealth and goods

By the use of a classroom activity this session introduces the children to some of the more nuanced and complex issues surrounding social justice and wealth distribution. This is where to go once you've exhausted fairness through cake sharing (see 'The Teddy Bears' Picnic' and 'Who Gets What? and Why?' in 'Links' below).

Equipment and preparation needed
- A set of 'vouchers' (these can be playing cards placed face down in the middle of the talk-circle – approximately as many as there are children in the classroom)
- Eight 'information cards' with the relevant information written on them (see below)

Key controversies
What is a just distribution of wealth/goods? Does dessert, need, equality or some other principle take priority over the others?

Subject links
Geography
Maths
PSHE

Possible misconception
That 'fair' simply means 'equal share'

Key concepts and vocabulary
Dessert   Fair   Need
Distribution Justice   Share
Equality

Key facilitation tool
Anonymity: putting on the ring of Gyges (see page 6)

Do: Place the vouchers on the floor in the middle of the talk-circle.

Say: I want you to imagine that you all live in a world where these vouchers are extremely valuable. With them you are able to get what you need and want. They are a little like money.

Task question: How will you distribute the vouchers among yourselves?

Nested questions
- How should you distribute the vouchers?
- Are there any rules about how you should distribute the vouchers?
- How should it be decided?
- Who should decide?
- How can it be policed? How should it be policed?

Do: Split the class into four groups – A, B, C, and D – of approximately equal size, though this is not necessary (in fact, as you will see, it could be interesting to leave one group larger or smaller than the others). Place a sheet of paper with the group's letter name beside them.

Say: Each of the groups A, B, C and D are small communities like a town or village. Each town wants to get as many of the vouchers as possible.

Repeat task question: How will you distribute the vouchers among yourselves?

Do: At some point during the discussion, randomly distribute four of the eight cards, giving one to each town.

Information cards:

1. Your town has a majority of disabled people.
2. Your town has a majority of people with a high IQ.
3. Your town has a majority of people with criminal backgrounds.
4. Your town has a majority of skilled labourers.
5. Your town has a majority of ethnic minorities.
6. Your town has a majority of immigrants.
7. Your town has a majority of poor people.
8. Your town has a majority of rich people.

Ask the task question again: How will you distribute the vouchers among yourselves?

Nested questions

- Does the information you now have change how you would or should distribute the vouchers?
- Are there any groups that have priority over others?
- Are you able to identify a principle that governs your decision? For instance, you may decide that *need* determines where the vouchers go? Or it could be *equality*, *merit*, *effort*, *talent*, *hierarchy* or *dessert*? Are there any others?

Put on the ring of invisibility

Here's how to apply the anonymity device (see Key Facilitation box on page 6).

1. Ask the children to imagine that they are invisible. Emphasise that they cannot get caught.

2. Give them each a piece of paper.

3. Ask them to write down, privately, how they would distribute the vouchers if they could take them without anyone knowing that it was them. Explain that no one will know what they wrote. They should not write their name on the piece of paper.

4. Collect the papers up. (I always have a box that I collect them in.)

5. Select one at random and enact what it says. So, if it says 'All the vouchers to go to town A', move all the vouchers to town A.

6. Read out the instruction you randomly selected, but do not reveal to the class who it was.

7. Share some of the other anonymous instructions.

Task question: ▶ **1a:** *Does* **'being invisible' change how you would distribute the vouchers?**

Task question: ▶ **1b:** *Should* **'being invisible' change how you would distribute the vouchers?**

Links

Once Upon an If: The Fair Well; The Two Sindbads; The Valley of the Diamonds

Philosophy for Young Children: The Teddy Bears' Picnic; The Animal Snack

The If Machine: Republic Island (vouchers could be adapted to be done as part of a series of Republic Island sessions); The Ring of Gyges

The If Odyssey: The Storyteller (for an example of self-anonymity)

The Philosophy Shop: Value; Politics, particularly A Fairer Society, Who Gets What? and Why?

POLES APART

Thinking about opposites

The Ancient Greek Presocratic philosophers' idea of 'the compresence of opposites' and the Chinese idea of 'Yin and Yang' both capture the way in which opposites have commonality as well as difference.

Equipment and preparation needed

- Have the poem ready to read
- Have the poem ready to project or hand out (optional)
- Read 'Simultaneous responses' in Appendix 1

Key controversies

Are opposites separated by difference or similarity? Do all things have an opposite?

Key concepts and vocabulary

Contradiction	In common	Share in
Contrary	Opposites	Similar
Different	Same	

Subject links

Literacy (logic, meaning)
Maths (logic)
PSHE

Possible misconception

That opposites have nothing in common

Key facilitation tool

Tension play

KEY FACILITATION TOOL

Tension play – using contradictions and contraries

It is tempting to smooth out contradictions in children's answers or, for instance, in information gathered on a board about something (such as an unknown number: 'the number must be even' and 'the number must be odd'), but one should resist doing this. Tensions, contradictions and contraries = learning opportunities. If someone contradicts themselves a 'response detector' (see in Appendix 1) is useful: 'Is there anyone who has something to say about that?' If two children, A and B, give the same reasons but reach *opposite* conclusions then, again, this is something you will want the whole class to think about. This can be done effectively by engaging A and B with each other: 'A, B just gave the same reasons as you, but B thought "not p" whereas you thought "p". Would you like to say anything about B's idea?' Sometimes, when children express themselves in, what *sounds* like, contradictions it may be that distinctions need to be drawn thereby exposing the apparent contradiction as an impostor. But whether or not what the children have said lead to contradictions or only *apparent* contradictions, these are in any case good opportunities for learning outcomes: if the children *reject* their positions because of contradictions or *refine* them with finely wrought distinctions.

DO: Before running this session read 'Simultaneous responses' in Appendix 1 and 'Approaching poetry' on page 2.

Say: I am going to read a poem called 'Poles Apart' that has missing words. You may shout out any single word you think should go in the missing spaces. Don't think too hard, just say a word! They could be rhyming words, but they don't have to be.

Poles Apart

What's the opposite of light?

_____.

What's the opposite of heavy?

_____.

Did you just say 'light'?
Can that be right?
Can one be the opposite of two?
And what's the opposite of me?

_____.

(Stop here and run Enquiry 1. There are plenty of questions already, so no task question should be required. Read the next part when you're ready.)

What's the opposite of black?

_____.

What's the opposite of blue?

_____.

What's the opposite of blind?

_____.

And alive?

_____.

ENQUIRY 2

 Do opposites have to be different?
Or do they have to be the same?
Are same and different the same or different?
Does opposite itself escape this game?

ENQUIRY 3

Task question: **What's the opposite of *opposite*?**

 One last riddle I think apposite
To help with your brain's general health:
Does the opposite of something's opposite
Always have to be itself?

ENQUIRY 4

Nested questions

- Is the opposite of something just its negation: X/not X?
- Which is the best opposite of light – 'dark' or 'not light'?
- Is 'not light' the same as 'dark'?
- Are there some things that have opposites?
- Are there some things that don't have opposites?

Links

Once Upon an If: The Square That Didn't Fit In; It

The If Machine: Thinking About Nothing; Goldfinger

The If Odyssey: Nobody's Home

The Philosophy Shop: Language and Meaning section, especially Tralse; Dizzy; Negative Nelly and The Accidental Confession; Itselfish; What We Talk About When We Talk About Words

Thoughtings: Chapter: Puzzles and Paradoxes

THE CONTRADICTION MONSTER

As with the previous Thought Adventure, this is a new Thoughting (a poem for thinking) for making sense of nonsense. It is a perfect companion session to Thought Adventure 5, Poles Apart.

Equipment and preparation needed

- Have the poem ready to read
- Have the poem ready to project or hand out (optional)
- Read 'Simultaneous responses' in Appendix 1

Key controversies

Are opposites separated by difference or similarity? Do all things have an opposite? 'Contradictions are true'; 'contradictions are false'. Are these two statements contradictory? Can contradictions be true?

Subject links

Literacy (logic, meaning)
Maths (logic)
PSHE

Possible misconception

That opposites have nothing in common.

Key concepts and vocabulary

Contradiction	In common	Share in
Contrary	Opposites	Similar
Different	Same	

Game: Opposites

Do:

This game can be used during this Thought Adventure or Thought Adventure 5.

1. Have the class stand up in a circle.
2. First: call out some words and have the class say, quickly – without thinking too much – the opposite of the word:

   - Light
   - Heavy
   - Now
   - Me
   - Everything
   - Top
   - Beauty
   - Three
   - Is
   - Zero
   - Different
   - Sea (see)
   - Any other words you can think of that would be interesting/obvious (mix them up)

3. Allow a discussion to follow the more contentious ones. Remember: you only need one person to say something different from everyone else for it to be contentious.
4. Next, or alternatively: go around the talk-circle and have each person say a word to which the entire class should respond with its opposite. The aim of this game is to try to think of something that has no opposite.

The Contradiction Monster (or, the poem that ends before it's begun!)

The contradiction monster
Is not like me and you
It does the strangest things, you know,
Things that we can't do.

It tips its hat, says, 'hello'
Then leaves as it arrives,
There's a pair of shoes on its only foot,
And no knife among its knives.

The contradiction monster
Is not as it appears,
When it comes to dinner
It gets smaller as it nears.

A mother with no children,
He sings to them at night.
The contradiction monster's wrong
Only when it's right.

Task question: **Does this poem make sense?**

Do: Go through each of the situations described with the class and see if they can 'get creative' and think of a situation in which the 'contradictory' statements could be true. For instance, is there a way, however strange and unlikely, for someone to have a pair of shoes on one foot? Can a mother be a he? Can you be wrong when you're right? Can you have no knife among your knives?

Explain what a contradiction is:

Say: A 'contradiction' is when you say something which you then cancel out by saying something else that makes what you said first not true. For example, 'Today is Christmas Day and today is not Christmas Day.'

Task question: **Are there any real contradictions in the poem?**

Spotting contradictions

Are these contradictions?

Remember: a contradiction is when *a statement is both true and false*. These accompanying guidance questions should help test for contradictions.

- This sentence is false.

  (Question: Is this sentence true and false?)

- 'I'm a liar!'

  (see 'The Liar's Paradox' on page 129. Question: Is the person who said this a liar and not a liar?')

- 'I didn't do nothing.'

  (Questions: Do you think that it's true that this person did and didn't do nothing?' See page 54)

- *The sun is out, the sky is blue*
  There's not a cloud to spoil the view
  But it's raining, raining in my heart.

  (From the song 'Raining in my heart' sung by Buddy Holly, written by Bryant and Bryant)

  (Question: Is it true that it is both sunny and not sunny in this song?)

- A: 'I don't want any more dinner, I'm not hungry'

  B: 'Do you want some pudding?'

  A: 'Yes please!'

  (Question: Do you think that it's true that A is both hungry and not hungry?)

Links

Once Upon an If: The Square That Didn't Fit In; It

The If Machine: Thinking About Nothing; Goldfinger

The If Odyssey: Nobody's Home

The Philosophy Shop: Language and Meaning section, especially Tralse; Dizzy; Negative Nelly and The Accidental Confession; Itselfish; What We Talk About When We Talk About Words

Thoughtings: Chapter: Puzzles and Paradoxes

THE GLASS OF WATER

Thinking about the power of the mind

This session serves as an introduction to Stoicism and Shakespeare, but also shows you, the teacher, a way of engaging primary-aged children with Shakespeare. See the end of the session for more Shakespeare suggestions.

Equipment and preparation needed

- A glass of water, half-filled
- Handouts or a projection of the extract from *Hamlet* (optional)

Subject links

Literacy
PSHE
Shakespeare

Key controversies

Is 'good and bad' a state of mind or a state of the world?

Key facilitation tool

Using false dichotomies

Key concepts and vocabulary

Attitude(s)	Negative	Pessimism
Bad	Optimism	Positive
Good	Perception	Value
Mental power		

KEY FACILITATION TOOL

Using false dichotomies

A false dichotomy is when a problem or situation is framed in terms of a choice between two things A or B but when there are alternatives (C, D, etc.) that have (usually deliberately) not been mentioned. As with 'Welcome assumptions' (see page 130) posing problems and situations in terms of a dichotomy *can* have the effect that it galvanises the children to seek alternatives, as well as making things easier by giving them a simple starting place: yes/no, true/false, A/B. Used judiciously, this can be a good thinking tool; its deliberate use to mislead, however, is naughty!

ENQUIRY 1: THE GLASS OF WATER

Do: Half fill a glass of water and place it in the middle of the talk-circle so all the children can see it. Then ask the following task question.

Task question: 1. Is the glass half full or is the glass half empty?

Nested questions

- Is there an answer to this question?
- Is it a matter of opinion?
- Can it be both?
- Is it good or bad that the glass is only half full/empty?

ENQUIRY 2: CONCEPTUAL APPLICATION EXERCISE

At some point it may become appropriate to introduce the following words. If so, write them up on the board:

• *Optimist*   • *Pessimist*

Find out if anyone has heard these words before, and see if anyone can explain the words to the class. Provide the following starting definitions, if they don't do so for themselves:

• An *optimist* is someone who sees things in a positive way; someone who often sees the good side of things.

• A *pessimist* is someone who sees things in a negative way; someone who often sees the bad side of things.

Questions:

• Which one, the optimist or the pessimist, would see the glass as half-full? Why?

• Which one, the optimist or the pessimist, would see the glass as half-empty? Why?

Task question: **2. Is it better to be an optimist or a pessimist?**

Nested questions

• Could there be an alternative position?

• Could the alternative position be better than either optimist or pessimist?

• Could one be *indifferent*? What does this mean?

ENQUIRY 3: HAMLET'S PRISON

Part one (Enquiries 1 and 2) makes a good session by itself. This second part is more advanced and can be approached in one of two ways: either use the full extract from *Hamlet* and allow the class to unpack it, or simply skip straight to the central *Hamlet* quote ('For there is nothing …'). The previous enquiry around the glass of water should have given the class what they need to approach the quote on their own. I recommend not explaining how the two parts link; give the class the opportunity to make the link. Because you want to get to *the thinking aspect* of the session I recommend not having members of the class read out the extract. I usually ask them to read it, dramatically, in pairs to each other; then I read it properly to the class as a whole and ask them to raise their hands if (among other things):

• There is a word they don't understand

• There is a phrase they don't understand

• They would like to say what they think the entire extract is about

• They would like to say what a particular part means

Give out the handouts or project the extract on the IWB, then read the following.

Say: This extract is taken from the play *Hamlet* by William Shakespeare (1557–1616) – it's the play that contains the line 'To be or not to be, that is the question'. This is another extract from the play that is less well known but is really good for thinking with.

Hamlet: Denmark's a prison.

Rosencrantz: Then is the world a prison?

Hamlet: A goodly one; in which there are many confines, wards and dungeons, Denmark being one of the worst.

Rosencrantz: [I] think not so my lord.

Hamlet: Why, then, 'tis no prison to you; for there is nothing either good or bad, but thinking makes it so: to me it is a prison.

Rosencrantz: Why then, your ambition makes it one; Denmark is too narrow for your mind.

Hamlet: I could be bounded in a nut shell and count myself a king of infinite space, were it not that I have bad dreams.

Once you have spent some time unpacking the extract, write up or project the following claim made by Hamlet:

Hamlet: Why, then, 'tis no prison to you; for there is nothing either good or bad, but thinking makes it so: to me it [Denmark] is a prison.

Do: If you are skipping to the single quote, write the following quote up on the board to begin Enquiry 3.

Say: *Hamlet: … for there is nothing either good or bad, but thinking makes it so …*

Do: First of all ask the class a hermeneutic question (see 'Question types' page xi): What do you think Hamlet means by this? Then ask the following task question.

Task question: **Do you agree with Hamlet – is it true that there is nothing either good or bad, but that thinking makes it so?**

Do: Ask the class to come up with some examples of things that are good or bad, no matter what you happen to think about them. Here are some situations you could share (use these examples if the children do not find their own, or to supplement the ideas they do come up with):

• You fail an exam.
• You win the lottery.
• Your family forget your birthday.
• Your tattooist misspells a word in your tattoo.
• Your favourite pet dies.
• You discover that you have become addicted to something.

EXTENSION ACTIVITY

Some history of philosophy

Depending on the age of the class you may decide to share the information below with them. Then take some of the quotes from below and ask the children to respond critically to them. You can do this by asking them if they agree or disagree with the quote.

Stoicism is a branch of Hellenistic (late Ancient Greek period, around 323–331 BCE) philosophy that derives its name from the 'painted porch' (*stoa poikile*) in the marketplace of Athens, under which many of the early Stoics taught. The school of Stoicism is said to have begun with Zeno of Citium (c. 334–262 BCE) and been further developed by Cleanthes of Assos (330–230 BCE) and Chrysippus of Soli (279–206 BCE). But the most famous of the Stoics are Epictetus (55–135 CE), originally a slave who later became a free man because of his philosophy; Seneca (4 BCE–65 CE), tutor and advisor to the Roman Emperor Nero; and Marcus Aurelius (121–180 CE), himself an Emperor of Rome (who features in the film *Gladiator*). The word 'stoic' has entered the English language and means 'to accept something undesirable without complaint'. The key ideas of stoicism are as follows (these can all be put to the children – see 'Quotes: Discuss' on page 80):

• All human beings have the capacity to attain happiness.
• Human beings are a 'connected brotherhood' and, unlike animals, are able to benefit each other rationally.
• Human beings are able to change their emotions and desires by changing their beliefs.
• Stoics care less about achieving something and much more about having done one's best to achieve it.
• Stoics attempt to understand what is in one's power and what is not, to act, when necessary, to change what it is in one's power to change, and to accept what it is not in one's power to change.

Epictetus

'It's not what happens to you, but how you react to it that matters.'

'The key is to keep company only with people who uplift you, whose presence calls forth your best.'

'There is only one way to happiness and that is to cease worrying about things which are beyond the power of our will.'

Seneca

'Most powerful is she who has herself in her own power.'

'As is a tale, so is life: not how long it is, but how good it is, is what matters.'

Marcus Aurelius

'The happiness of your life depends upon the quality of your thoughts.'

'Everything we hear is an opinion, not a fact.'

'Our life is what our thoughts make it.'

More philosophy through Shakespeare's ideas

Make use of PaRDeS (see Appendix 2) for the following, and adapt as necessary.

- Macbeth's 'She should have died hereafter' speech from *Macbeth*.

Task question: What, if anything, does life signify (mean)?

- Hamlet's 'To be, or not to be' speech from *Hamlet*.

Task question: What is the question? What is the answer?

- Prospero's 'Our revels now are ended' speech from *The Tempest*.

Task question: Task question: Are we such stuff as dreams are made on?

- Claudio's 'Ay, but to die speech' from *Measure For Measure*.

Task question: What is it to die? Should we fear death?

See also Epicurus's argument for why we shouldn't fear death.

- Falstaff's 'Honour pricks me on' speech in *Henry IV Part 1*.

Task question: What is honour? Is it good to be honourable?

Links

The Philosophy Shop: The Traffic Light Boy sessions

The Saddest King by Chris Wormall

Thoughtings: Bite; Happy Sad

IS THIS A POEM?

Thinking about poetry

Approaching poetry and engaging students with poetry is always a challenge for teachers, but one way to do so is to invite students to think about what poetry is (and what it's not).

Equipment and preparation needed
- A whiteboard and board pens
- Have the poems 'A Shopping List?' and 'Am I a Poem?' ready to project or hand out

Subject links
Literacy (poetry)

Key controversies
Can poetry be clearly defined? What is and what is not poetry?

Key facilitation tool
Anchoring (see page 7)

Key concepts and vocabulary

Couplet	Poetry	Scan
Form	Prose	Simile
Line	Rhyme	Stanza
Metaphor	Rhythm	

KEY FACILITATION TOOL

Anchor

See also 'Anchoring' on page 7. In this session, the key question is: 'What is a poem?' So when the children answer the task question 'Is it a poem?', in order to encourage the students to make their answer relevant and informative, it will often (though not always) need to be anchored to the main question: 'So, if it is not a poem then what is a poem and why?' Or if the task question is: 'Does a poem have to rhyme?' and the answer is 'no', anchor like so: 'So, if a poem doesn't need to rhyme what does a poem need, if anything?' If you continue anchoring throughout the session you are much more likely to have a rich list of possible necessary features of a poem, and (probably) many of them will be what you were meant to teach that day, such as *rhyme* and *rhythm* and possibly a few extras too, such as *artistic intention* or *free verse*.

Say: Today's question doesn't come from me; it comes from a … well, that's just it – that's what we're going to have to investigate.

Do: Write this up on the board:

 Is This A Poem?

Anchor the children (see page 7, and box) to the poem's question, making sure you open them up (see Appendix 1).

- If they say 'yes' then ask, 'Why is it a poem?'
- If they say 'no' ask them, 'Why is it not a poem?'
- In order to begin drawing up a definition of poetry with the class, always follow up with this task question:

Task question: **If this is not a poem, then what is a poem?**

Do: Record the answers on the board using a concept-map (see page 88).

Nested questions

- Is 'Is This a Poem?' a poem or not?
- If so, why? If not, why not?
- What if it was written out like this: Is this a poem?
- Or backwards: ?meop a siht sI
- How many different ways can this poem be presented?
- What is a poem?
- What if it was called (and read) 'This Is a Poem' – would it be a poem then?
- And what if it was called (and read) 'This Is Not a Poem' – would it be a poem then, or not?
- What about 'I Am a Poem.' Or 'Am I a Poem?' (See 'Am I a Poem?' on the next page)

EXTENSION ACTIVITY

Borderline cases

Here are some more examples of short poems.

Mattina
M'illumino d'immenso
                        (Ungaretti)

Task question: **Can you translate 'Mattina' from Italian into English?**

Fleas   *Me*
Adam   *We*
Had 'em   *(Muhammed Ali)*
          (anonymous)
                                 Three Things I hate
Poet   *Hate*
Poet?   *Lists*
Know it!   *Irony*
          (Peter Worley)   *(A variation by Peter Worley on popular Internet posts)*

Task question: **Are the above examples poems?**

Shopping list?

Shopping List A	Shopping List B
Cereal	Cereal
String	String
Strawberries	Strawberries
Flour	Flour
Pots	Pots
Toms	Toms
Cream (sour)	Cream (sour)

Task question: If one of these was written to be a poem and the other was written to be a shopping list, are either of them poems?

Nested questions

- Go through your list of features of poetry (see concept-map instruction). Does 'Shopping List A or B' have any of the features you listed? For example, does it rhyme? Does it have rhythm?

- Is there any perceptible difference between the two examples?

- Is there any (non-perceptible) difference between the two examples?

- What is a 'non-perceptible difference'? Does it make sense?

- Does the *intention* of the writer make any difference as to whether it's a poem or a shopping list? If it is a significant difference, is *intention* a 'perceptible' or 'non-perceptible' difference?

Am I a Poem?

I am a poem
Though you may not agree
I rhyme and have rhythm
And a little imagery:
'Like a small framed painting'
– Or at least I do now.
It's a simile as well,
To make you go 'Wow!'

Task question: Is 'Am I a Poem?' a poem?

Nested questions

- The poem says that it has rhyme, rhythm, imagery and a simile. Is the poem right? Check to see if it has these features. If it does, does that make it a poem?

- If the poem says that it's a poem, does that mean that it is a poem? Compare this with:
  - If you say that you're a girl, does that mean that you are a girl?
  - If you say that you are saying something, does that mean that you are saying something?
  - If you ask your smartphone if it's happy and it says 'yes', does that mean that it is happy?

- Is the poem 'Am I a Poem?' cheating? If so, in what way?

Shortings

Thoughtings are poems written to get you thinking. A *shorting* is a *Thoughting* for the Twitter generation, written to get you thinking in 140 characters or less. Here are a couple of examples.

Space To Think

Nospacetothinkmakesnosense
Space to think makes sense.
B ut notw hen thes p ace s
A r ei nthew ron gp lac e s.

See 'The ghost' (page 1) for a model for approaching the interpretation of poems, and see also PaRDeS (Appendix 2) for some ideas of how to put a poem like this to the children.

Sort of

I could of. I should of. Would I of? Sort of. But could of is sort of short of should of.
So did I?
I – sort of just short of – did.

Task question: Did whoever it is do whatever it is they're talking about doing?

Nested questions

- Can you read the poem out loud, replacing the incorrect words with the correct words?
- Should all the 'of's be replaced with 'have's?
- What's the difference between 'short of' and 'short for'? Which one is being used in the poem?
- What does 'sort of just short of did' mean?
- In what way is 'could of' short of 'should of'?

Do: Have the children write their own *shortings* (in 140 characters or less).

Links

The Philosophy Shop: Philosophical Poetry; Said and Unsaid; What We Talk About When We Talk About Words
Thoughtings: Puzzles, Problems and Paradoxes in Poetry to Think With by Peter Worley and Andrew Day

THE DOG THAT MEOWED

Thinking about identity

This new Thoughting provides a lighthearted way to tackle some of the more difficult aspects of personal identity.

Equipment and preparation needed
- Have the poem ready to hand out or project on the board.

Subject links
Literacy
PSHE

Key controversies
What determines what something is? Do looks or behaviour matter more when determining what something is?

Possible misconception
That one's identity is determined only by physical attributes

Key facilitation tool
Carve it up! (see below)

Key concepts and vocabulary
Behaviour
Biology
Gender
Identity

Inside/Outside
Looks
Self-conception
Sex

KEY FACILITATION TOOL

Carve it up!

Listen out for clue-phrases that suggest distinctions need to be made in order for the discussion to progress. If, in answer to the question 'Is he free?' some of the children say things like, 'In a way yes and in a way no because …' or 'I think both yes and no' or 'I think 50/50', and so on, then they are probably sensitive to the fact (though not necessarily consciously aware of it) that there's more than one meaning of the word 'free' in play. When you hear clue-phrases like these, ask the following question to encourage the children to begin drawing their own distinctions: 'Do you think that there is more than one kind of X?' or 'Do you think that there is more than one way in which you can be X?' Often in discussions, until a distinction has been drawn, the discussion will go in circles. Also, this is one of the key ways in which you can achieve a positive outcome from a philosophy discussion: the class may not have answered the question about whether something is the same thing as it continues through time, but, along the way, they may well have established that there are different uses of the word 'same'. This is important conceptual learning. In this session, children often draw a distinction between two identity determinants: *what you are on the outside* and *what you are on the inside*. Everything that is said about dogs and cats may also be pertinent to people with regard to gender, for example. (See 'A next step' on page 32.)

DO: Read the following *Thoughting* first:

> **The Dog That Meowed**
>
> *Dogs bark!*
> *Mice squeak!*
> *Angels hark!*
> *People speak!*
> *They're among the first things you learn*
>
> *I have a dog, though,*
> *That sounds a sound*
> *Which may cause some concern*
>
> *Because my dog meows*
> *When he opens his snout*
> *And does what should be a 'woof',*
>
> *On the outside*
> *My dog is a dog*
> *But inside*
> *He's not cat enough!*

Task question: **Is it a dog or a cat?**

Nested questions

- When is a dog not a dog? (This makes the assumption that it is possible for a dog not to be a dog – see 'Welcome assumptions' on page 130.)
- When is a dog a cat?
- Can a dog be a cat on the inside?
- Can a cat be a dog on the outside?
- When is a cat a cat?
- When is a dog a dog?
- What is a cat?
- What is a dog?
- Can something other than a dog/cat be a dog/cat?
- If you have something that *looks* like a dog but *acts* like a cat, is it a dog or a cat?
- Is there a difference between a cat that looks like a dog and a dog that acts like a cat?

Enquiry on identity more generally

1. Start off by writing up 2 = 2 on the board, and ask the following task question:

Task question: ⟩ **1. Is this true?**

2. Place two chairs side by side, and ask:

Task question: ⟩ **2. Are they identical?**

3. Then ask:

Task question: ⟩ **3. Are the chairs identical to themselves?**

4. Refer the class to Shakespeare's character Iago from his play *Othello*. Don't tell them anything about the character until they've reflected on what he might mean (see step 5, below).

5. Write up on the board Iago's line 'I am not what I am.'

6. Then ask the hermeneutic question: What do you think Iago might mean?

Final task question:

Task question: ⟩ **4. Are you identical to yourself?**

A next step

'The Dog That Meowed' allows a discussion of gender-related issues at something of a distance. 'Who Decides?' brings the issue closer to the class. So, if your class make the leap themselves, or if you wish to do so (and are comfortable doing so) then read the following poem:

Who Decides?

Who decides if I'm tall or short?
Or what colour eyes I peer from?

Who decides what clothes I wear,
Or if I'll choose the blue or pink one?

Who decides what films I like?
Or what my favourite song is?

And who decides what job I'll take?
And whether I'm Mr or Mrs?

Nested questions

- How many people are involved in the decision?
- Does being a girl or boy determine whether you will choose pink or blue?
- Can you choose the colour of your eyes, or how tall or short you are?
- Can you choose what films you like?
- Can you choose your sex?
- Can you choose your gender?
- What is the difference between sex and gender? (This could be a research question – see page 119.)

Links

Once Upon an If: Once Upon an If (part 1); The Boy With No Name; The Cat That Barked

The If Machine: The Android; Where Are You?; The Ship of Theseus

The If Odyssey: The Storyteller; The Stranger

The Philosophy Shop: James and Jemima; Pinka and Arwin Go Forth: Different Animals?

Thoughtings: 'Puzzles and Paradoxes'; 'You, Me, Aliens and Others'

IF A ROCKSLIDE TUMBLES ON AN ISLAND

Thinking about reality, perception and definitions

It's taken me this long to put this famous philosophical question into one of my books, but seeing as it keeps coming up in the classroom, I had to. But here's a question for you: is it a philosophy question, a science question, or both?

Equipment and preparation needed
• None

Subject links
Science (sound)

Key controversies
Does the concept of *sound* include 'the *interpretation* of vibrating airwaves'? Can a noise or sound happen if there is nothing to sense the vibration?

Key concepts and vocabulary
Hear

Noise

Sound

Interpretation

Objective causes of sound (see dictionary definition, below)

Perception

Subjective experience of sound (see dictionary definition, below)

Possible misconception
That a sensation is the same as the objective, causal features of the sensation

Key facilitation tool
Iffing (see page 36)

Say: I want you to imagine a place, somewhere on this planet, that is completely uninhabited; maybe a small rocky island somewhere near the Antarctic. There are absolutely no people or living things of any kind. Suddenly, a rockslide happens. The rocks tumble down a dusty slope and come to rest on the beach.

Task question: There is no one around to hear the rockslide, so does the rockslide make any sound?

Nested questions
• What is sound?
• Is sound something that happens independently from our minds?
• Does sound require interpretation?

- There's no one around to see the rockslide, so does that mean that the rockslide does not happen? Is there a difference between this question and the main task question?
- With no one around, does the air still move when the rocks tumble?
- With no one around can the moving air be translated into sound?
- Is sound the same as noise?
- Does the dictionary help to solve the problem?
    - *Definition 1a*: the sensation perceived by the sense of hearing.
    - *Definition 1c*: the objective cause of hearing: energy that is produced by a vibrating body, [that] is transmitted by longitudinal waves of pressure that travel outwards from the source through a medium (e.g. air). – *Longman's Dictionary of the English Language*
- Could the answer be *no*, according to definition 1a, and *yes*, according to definition 1c? If so, this problem is an example of a problem that *can* be solved by drawing some nuanced distinctions (see 'Carve it up!' on page 30).

EXTENSION ACTIVITY

The dark side of Pluto

Say: This time, I want you to imagine a place on the dark side of a distant planetary body such as Pluto, or even a comet. Imagine a rockslide happening there. On this planetary body there is, unlike on Earth, no air.

Task question: **On the dark side of Pluto there are no people or living creatures of any kind and there is no air, so does the rockslide make any sound?**

Nested question

- Is air necessary for sound to occur? (This makes a good research question – see page 119.)

Do: Once this enquiry is finished, return to the first enquiry.

Links

The If Machine: The Chair (particularly the 'asteroid' scenario at the end)
The Philosophy Shop: The Sound of Silence; Music To My Ears; The Piano Music

Iffing

This is a form of questioning that makes use of the conditional sentence structure 'if … then …' in order to engender hypothetical thinking. For example, '*If* a tree falls in a forest and there is no one around to hear it, *then* does it make a sound?' Making use of the iffing strategy in your questioning helps to do the following:

- Avoid factual obstacles to a discussion ('If we could swap brains then where would Jenny and Alma be? – see 'Where Are You?' in *The If Machine*)

- Keep the discussion conceptual

- Test ideas against the task question ('If [child's idea] unicorns are not real then [task question] how many horns do they have?')

- Consider alternative points of view or possibilities ('If unicorns are not real, then …'; 'And if unicorns are real, then …')

Ropes and hoops

Asking children to categorise things is a useful way to explore a problem, to solve problems by drawing distinctions (see 'Carve it up!' on page 30), and to see where there might be some grey areas. There is a categorisation exercise in 'Reality glasses' (page 119), where the children are invited to divide things up into two sets: 'real' and 'not real'. You could use rope or hoops placed on the floor to form circles in which the children can place objects or cards/boards with words on. Using different-sized ropes and hoops, the children are encouraged to find subsets, and to overlap between sets. For instance, you could do a *same or different?* categorisation exercise on shapes with two hoops, with one labelled 'same as a square' and the other 'different from a square'. At first, one of the children might put a circle in the 'different' hoop and another square in the 'same' hoop, but then struggle to decide where to put a rectangle. Is it *same* or *different*? What the child needs is a new category, *similar*, but what the child might do – being without this third category – is to overlap the hoops and place the rectangle in the overlapped segment. Or, they may place the rectangle *between* the hoops.

Ropes and hoops

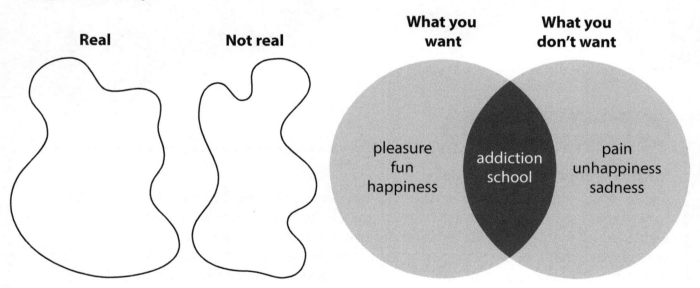

THE MAYBE CAT

Thinking about uncertainty

Inspired by the famous 'Schrodinger's cat' thought experiment and containing two new Thoughtings, I have found this session to engender some great discussions around reality, possibility and – to use a classic philosophical expression – thereness.

Equipment and preparation needed
- A non-transparent box
- Sticky tape
- A hand-drawn picture of a cat (or not – see below)
- Have poems ready for projection or to hand out

Subject links
Literacy
Science

Key controversies
Is there a state between being and not being?

Key concepts and vocabulary
Alternatives	Might
Contingency	Possibility
Knowledge	The subjunctive
Maybe	There (being)

Key facilitation tool
Introduce appropriate new ideas

KEY FACILITATION TOOL

Introduce appropriate new ideas

The American author, physician and poet, Oliver Wendell Holmes (1809–1894) said, 'A man's mind, stretched by a new idea, can never go back to its original dimensions.' When working with children, this can be a warning and a recommendation. It's a warning not to push ideas onto children that they are not ready for, or that might disturb them. I would not, for instance, run a session for primary school children using the device of Descartes's 'evil demon' thought-experiment from his *Meditations*, as it has the potential to disturb in a way that would be inappropriate for children. The quote acts as a recommendation, however, to – on occasion – put suggestions to children so that they are opened up to possibilities they are not likely to think of on their own, thereby allowing the students to 'stretch' their minds over a new idea. If I do this (though I find that I seldom need to when the children are properly facilitated) I do so with multiple-choice lists such as the one in this session. However, you must always wait to see what they come up with first, giving the class the chance to say what you would have said. Simply add what they don't mention to the list, if you need to.

The preparation for this session should be done at home before going to school. Of course, you don't need to do any of this; you could just draw a picture of a cat and put it in the box, but, by doing all of this prep, it adds psychological authenticity to the session as well as making the session more interesting for you.

Do: Give the box and the piece of paper to a friend or another member of your family. Read the following to them:

Say: I want you either to draw a picture of a cat, or not; you decide. Then, either place it in the box, or not. Again, you decide. Then, seal the box with tape, and – whatever you do – don't tell me what you did!

Do: When this has been done, take the box, with its mysterious contents (or not!) to school. When you are ready to run the session, place the box in the middle of the room and explain, carefully and clearly, what you said to your friend/family member. Then ask this question:

Task question: 1. **What are the possibilities of what's in the box?**

The students should come up with something like the following:

• There's nothing in the box.
• There's a blank piece of paper in the box.
• There's a piece of paper with a picture of a cat on it.
• And so on …

Be prepared for some interesting suggestions, such as that there is a picture of something else entirely in the box. As the instruction was to 'draw a picture of a cat or not', 'or not' could be interpreted in a number of ways: either simply 'not drawing anything' or 'drawing something else not mentioned'. So, don't limit their list to what I've got above or to what you expect. This is an interesting exercise in *sets* and *subsets* of 'not' and 'nothing' as well as 'something'.

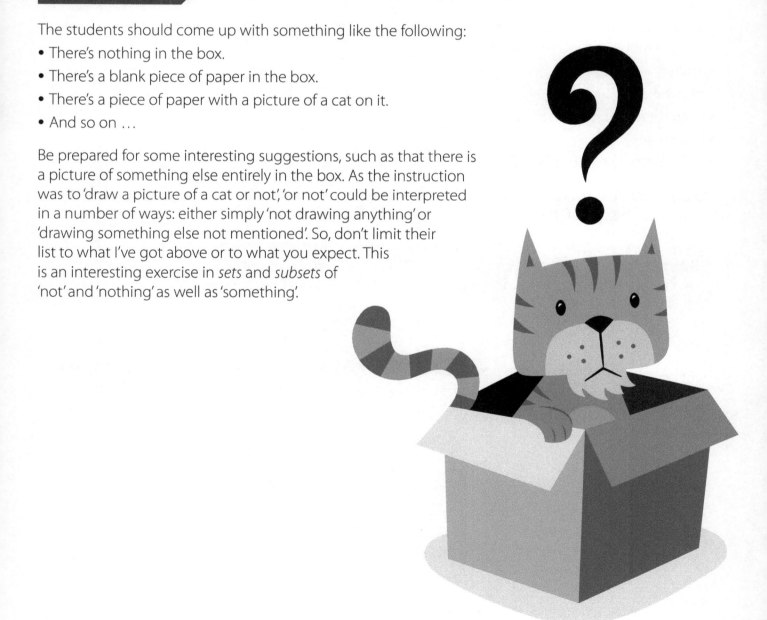

Task question: Task question: 2. Before we open the box, is the drawing of the cat there?

Nested questions

- Usually, we say that something 'is there' or that something 'is not there'. Is there something else, something different to 'there' or 'not there'?
- Is a table *there*?
- Is an imaginary table *there*?
- Is a thought *there*?
- Is a memory *there*?
- What is *there*? (What does the word 'there' do? When we use the word 'there' what are we doing with it?) Repeat these questions but replace the word 'there' with 'might'. And then again with 'real'.
- What is 'maybe'? How does the word 'maybe' work?
- What is 'possible'? How does the word 'possible' work?

If necessary, you could make some suggestions for TQ2 to open their minds to possibilities they may not have thought of on their own:

- There?
- Not there?
- Both there *and* not there?
- Half there?
- Or something else not listed?

Note: As with 'The hypothesis box' session (see page 90), it is always interesting to ask the following question at the end of the session to see how the children respond.

Say: Should we open the box to see what's in it, if anything, or do you think that it would spoil the philosophical aims of the session if we did?

Those who opt not to open the box, I believe, display a degree of intellectual maturity that is perhaps beyond their years. I should point out that I'm not suggesting that those who opt to open it are intellectually immature.

Here are two new *Thoughtings* to take this session further:

Monster Under The Bed?

There might *be a monster under my bed,*
It might *be vicious, or funny instead,*
Might *want to eat every last bit of me,*
Might *want a friend,*
Might *be lonely.*

Might *have claws;*
Might *be shy;*
Might *have a tail*
And just one eye;
Might *be massive;*
Might *be small –*
So small,
Can't see it at all.

Might *be long;*
Might *be fat;*
Might *be as big*
As an averaged-sized cat;
Might *be hungry,*
And –
I already said –
There might *be a monster*
Under my bed.

There might *be a monster by my duvet*
Might *be waiting to give me a scare*
But a monster that might *be*
Can't take me away,
Coz a monster that might *be's*
Only half there.

Task question: ▶ **Can something be 'half there'?**

(See Nested questions for TQ2.)

> **Monster Under The Bed.**
>
> *There's* definitely *a child on the bed*
> *That I sit under, that covers my head,*
> *That hides me from the world of people,*
> *That keeps us monsters mythical,*
> *That makes us only* might *be here*
> *To the children out there who* think *they hear*
> *A monster's slow, rasping breath …*
>
> *And because we only* might *be here*
> *It scares them half to death!*

Comprehension questions:

- Who or what is speaking in this poem?
- What is the speaker saying?

Nested questions

- What's scarier, a monster that is there or a monster that only might be there?
- So, is the monster there?
- How can you be scared of something that isn't there? (Or doesn't exist?)
- How can a fictional monster have a point of view? (See 'Perspectacles' on page 122.)
- Do fictional creatures exist? (Are they there?)
- Do mythical creatures exist? (Are they there?)
- What is fictional? What is mythical? What's the difference?

Links

Once Upon an If: It

The If Machine: The Little Old Shop of Curiosities

The If Odyssey: Nobody's home; Under The World; The Horror of The Rocks

The Philosophy Shop: Metaphysics: Fiction; The Confession; Tina's Ghost; The Otherwise Machine; What Zeus Does When He's Bored; The Butterfly Effect

Thoughtings: Possible World?; The Stone

THE BOOK OF EVERYTHING

Thinking about everything

This session deals with everything, but if you think 'everything' means 'everything', think again! It's what's not in the book of everything that sometimes surprises. I recommend making use of the ideas in 'Ropes and hoops' (see page 37) for this session.

Equipment and preparation needed
- A large book (optional)
- Some ropes and/or hoops

Key controversies
What would be included in a list of everything? Is nothing part of everything? Do non-things feature as part of everything? What is a thing?

Subject links
Literacy
Science

Key facilitation tool
Ropes and hopes (see page 37)

Key concepts and vocabulary
Everything
Knowledge and its limits
Universality
Universe

Do: Place the large book on the floor in the centre of the talk-circle.

Say: Imagine that this book is huge, because it's a book of everything; a book with everything in it.

Do: Read the following new *Thoughting*:

The Book of Everything

Imagine a book, just for a minute,
With nothing left out; with everything in it
All lists, and all numbers, though they be infinite,
Would have to be there, though they don't fit in it.

How would you write it, or read it or bring it?
How would you finish or even begin it?
And if, as a prize, you were to win it,
Don't read it – just bin it!
Coz it would be so boring.
Innit?!

Do: Ask the following questions reasonably successively, though with enough time to explore the first a little.

Task question: 1. What would be in the book of everything?

Task question: 2. What would *not* be in the book of everything?

Nested questions

- What is everything?
- Would the Book of Everything be in itself?
- Is nothing part of everything?
- Is there anything that is not part of everything?
- Is 'not everything' part of everything or not?
- Are things we don't know part of everything?
- Is the future part of everything?
- Are people that haven't been born yet part of everything?
- Are words that haven't been made up yet part of everything?
- Can we ever *know* everything?
- Is heaven part of everything?

Task question: 3. What does the word 'everything' include?

Say: Imagine writing a list of everything and imagine writing a list of what would be in the Book of Everything.

Task question: 4. Is there anything that would be on one list but not on the other?

EXTENSION ACTIVITY

Anything, something, nothing and everything

Put a variety of objects on the floor for all to see; four or five objects should do it.

1. Ask someone to pick nothing up.
2. Ask someone to pick everything up.
3. Ask someone to pick anything up.
4. Ask someone to pick something up.

Task question: 1. Does 'anything' mean the same as 'something'?

Task question: 2. Does 'anything' mean the same as 'everything'?

How to know everything

Another *Thoughting*; one that inspired one of my favourite arguments from an eight-year-old: 'If there is anything that can't exist,' she said, 'it exists, so there can't be anything that can't exist.'

> *How to know everything*
>
> *Is there any question that can't be answered?*
> *Is there any fact that can't be known?*
> *Is there any idea that can't be said?*
> *Is there anything that can't be thought?*
> *Is there anything that can't be experienced?*
> *Is there anything that can't be imagined?*
> *Is there anything that can't exist?*
> *Answer each of these questions,*
> *Add the list of things that* can't be *to the list of things that* can,
> *Know the full list of things that* can't be *and the things that* can,
> *Then, at long last, you will know* everything.

No task question is usually needed for this, as it is full of questions that should elicit some responses, and an argument at the end to agree or disagree with. If you must:

Task question: Is the poet right, is that how you would know everything?

The Hodja's First Day Teaching

This is an original story adapted from Plato's *Meno* dialogue, and it represents what is known as *the paradox of enquiry*. It raises the question: can we really ever learn anything new or find out what we don't know?

This is a dialogue story, so that it can be performed by two class members either as a first reading and/or a second reading.

Do: Begin by reading the introduction passage to 'The Hodja' (see page 72), then read the story. Stop to enquire at any appropriate time during the dialogue; you don't have to read it all through first.

Say:

It was the Hodja's first day as a teacher.

'Before I can tell you what I need to teach you, I need to ask: what don't you know?' he began.
'There's lots of stuff we don't know, sir,' said a pupil to the Hodja.
'Good. What is it?' he asked.
'Well, we don't know because we don't know it,' she said.
'Let's find it out then!' replied the Hodja, cheerfully.
'How will we do that?' said the pupil.
'We will enquire together,' said the Hodja.
'But what are we looking for?' she asked.
'I don't know because we haven't found it yet,' said the Hodja, 'so let's get on with it and start looking!'
'But you must tell us what we are looking for,' insisted the pupil, 'or else we won't know what it is if we find it.'
'But how can we enquire into what it is we don't know if we already know what it is?' said the Hodja. He was beginning to confuse himself.
'Errrmm ...' said the pupil, also a little confused.
'Come on! Let's not waste any more time. Let's start enquiring so we can find things out,' said the Hodja. He was beginning to realise that teaching wasn't as easy as he had thought.
'OK!' said the pupil, finally convinced, 'Where do we start?'
'Errrrmmm ...' said the Hodja.

Task question: How should they begin?

Nested questions
- When will their enquiry end?
- How do you begin finding out what you don't know?
- How will you know when you know it?
- If you don't know something, then how would you know if you found it?
- If you do know something, then is there any point in enquiring into it?
- What is enquiry?
- What is learning?
- How do we acquire knowledge?
- How do teachers teach?
- Is there a good way to teach? Is there a bad way to teach?
- Can you make sense of the discussion?

Links

Once Upon an If: The Six Wise Men; The Cat That Barked

The If Machine: Get Stuffed; To The Edge of Forever; The Little Old Shop of Curiosities; Thinking About Nothing

The If Odyssey: Nobody's Home; Under The World

The Philosophy Shop: Metaphysics (many entries, particularly 'Ontology' and 'Fiction')

SENTENCES

Thinking about meaning, structure and relationships

Colleagues I've shared this with have all said that this session needs to be seen, so please visit (http://www.philosophy-foundation.org/resources/40) to see a demonstration of this rich session for numercy and literacy. One of the most important sessions I think I've developed, so I had to include it.

Equipment and preparation needed

- Prepare an array of contrasting kinds of symbols on pieces of A4 paper or card (it is better if the card is thick enough that the children cannot see through it). For example:
  - Numbers 1–10 (each number on a separate piece of paper) – maybe '0' too
  - All the operations: x, -, +, ÷, = (again, each on a separate piece of paper) plus two sets of brackets '(', ')', '(', ')'
  - Some shapes: a square, a circle, a triangle (on separate pieces of paper)
  - Some pictures: a picture of a cat, a picture of a stick man, a picture of a cake, a picture of half a cake, etc.
  - Some sums: '1 + 1 + 1', '2 + 2', etc.
  - Some words: 'cat', 'man', 'one', 'three', 'shape', etc.
  - Definitions/descriptions: of a cat, of a square, of a cake, etc.
- Place all the prepared cards with symbols on face down, on the floor, inside the talk-circle
- Have five cards with a '?' on, to act as place-holders
- You could also have some colours, letters, emojis or musical notes …

Key controversies

Can mathematical sentence structures be used with non-maths values? If so, how can they? What are sentences, exactly?

Key concepts and vocabulary

Function	Sentences
Meaning	Structure
Operations	Value
Relationships	

Key facilitation tool

Web of understanding (see page 52)

Subject links

Literacy
Maths

You can do whatever you like with these symbols, once you've got them, to help the children explore the nature of meaning, structure and relationships. However, to get you started, here are some enquiry suggestions using the symbols suggested above.

Do: Place your five place-holder cards on the floor. I've said five here because that gives standard sums such as 2 + 2 = 4, but it could be any number of place-holder cards:

ENQUIRY 1: FINDING MEANING, CREATING MEANING

Do: Ask a child to come up and randomly select a face-down piece of paper and put it in the place of a '?', then ask another child to do the same. Carry on until all the question marks have been replaced with randomly selected symbols, for example:

'1 + 1 + 1', , 'dog', +, 10

Task question: **1. Does this 'sentence' make sense?**
(This is the question you should *anchor* to a good deal in this session.)

Task question: **2. Is it possible to make the sentence make sense by moving the cards around?**

Do: Repeat this exercise as many times as necessary or desired, randomly creating sentences for the class to interpret or move around.

The sense test
Throughout this session, use the following test to see if something makes sense. If the 'sentence' makes sense, the class should be able to say what it means. The more ambiguous the sentence, the more wide-ranging the interpretations are likely to be. Whenever someone constructs a sentence, ask them not to say what it means until you've heard a few ideas from the class about what they think it says. Only then have them say what they intended it to express.

ENQUIRY 2: WHAT IS A SENTENCE?

Say (at an appropriate time)**:** I've been calling these [indicate an example of structured symbols on the floor] 'sentences'. Are they sentences?

Task question: **3. Are they *sentences*?**

Nested questions
- Can you explain why or why not?
- What is it for something to make sense?
- Are the words 'sentence' and 'sense' related? (This is a good research question (see page 119).)

Do: Write up an example of what the children say to test their ideas against their intuitions. So …

- If someone says that a sentence 'begins with a capital letter and ends with a full stop', then write 'P.' on the board and ask TQ4 again.
- If someone then says that a sentence 'has to contain a verb' then write 'P go.' (One girl said that this is a sentence if 'P' is somebody's name.)
- If someone says that a sentence is 'a group of words all together', ask for some random words from the class and write them on the board in no particular order but making sure that they are 'together' in some way.
- Carry on in this way, anchoring back to TQ4 each time until they move to a more satisfactory definition of a sentence.

To help bring out any possible controversies, test their definition against unusual examples from the session such as 'picture sentences', 'mixed sentences' (arithmetic and words), 'people sentences' and so on. For example, say: 'So, if a sentence is "a string of words that are meaningful" how were you able to make a sentence out of yourselves? Was what you made not a sentence or can a sentence be made without words?'

ENQUIRY 3: SEEING MEANING

Try out some of the following sentences and others that you have created:

- $3 = 1 + 1 + 1$

- ▢ + ▷ + ◯ = 'shapes'

- ▢ + ▷ = 'house'

- 🍰 + 🧍 = 😀 (Question: is the = sign being used in the same way here as described in 'Identity parade', below? If not, what's different about its use here?)

ENQUIRY 4: COMPLETING MEANING

Ask the children to complete the following sentences:

- 'picture of cake', divided sign, 4, = ?
- 'pic of dog', +, 'pic of cat' = ?
- ?, +, 2, =, 43
- 'divided sign', ?, = 1 'man' = ?

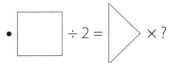

When I put this sum out, Dylan, aged eight, simply drew a line through the square and labelled one half '1' and the other '2' then added a '2' at the end:

ENQUIRY 5: IDENTITY PARADE

Do: Ask them what '=' means. Explore and concept-map their answers (see page 88).

Say: '=' means 'identical' or 'the same as'. So, do these sentences make sense?

- ☐ = 'square' = 'a closed, plain figure with 4 straight, equal lines connected by right angles'
- 1 + 1 + 1, = 3
- 3, =, 1+1+1
- =, =, 'the same as'
- =, 'the same as', =
- 'the same as', =, =

ENQUIRY 6: MAKING SENSE

Do: Give students blank pieces of paper and ask them to construct their own sentences, using the existing symbols, but writing new ones if necessary. Set a variety of different tasks, such as:

- Create a sentence using mathematical operations (x, -, +, ÷, =) but no numbers (so, pictures, shapes, words, but not words of numbers etc.)
- Create a sentence with only pictures.
- Create a sentence using themselves. (One class I did this with used bodily and facial expressions to communicate a sentence to the class, very successfully.)
- Create a sentence that everyone understands in the same way using only pictures and operations. (Use 'The sense test' – see box on page 48.)
- A picture sentence that ends with 'pic of triangle'.
- A number sentence that ends with '4'.
- A colour sentence that ends with 'blues'.
- A word sentence that ends with 'cube'.

EXTENSION ACTIVITY

Literacy sentences

Devise and run a similar session following the same kinds of enquiry ideas as above, around English sentences. Use simple propositions such as 'it is raining' and 'snow is white', connectives such as 'and', 'or', 'because', 'so' 'if … then …', 'if and only if'; then add whatever you need, such as some adjectives, nouns, verbs, negations, etc. Try mixing them up, as above, with pictures, numbers, maths and so on.

Links

Once Upon an If: The Cat That Barked; The Promise Slippers

The If Machine: Goldfinger; The Shadow of the Pyramid

The If Odyssey: Clouded

The Numberverse by Andrew Day: This and That Make Ten; Inbetweeny Bits; Bone Setting; The Real Deal; Two Square Thoughts

The Philosophy Shop: Language and Meaning

Thoughtings: Word Wonders; Poems To Do; Number Wonders; Puzzles and Paradoxes

TPF website: 'Tabby Is a Cat' by Andrew Day

Web of understanding

When using enquiries you should not be teaching, but facilitating. This does not mean, however, that teaching and facilitation are two separate things that never-the-twain shall meet. Enquiries afford many opportunities for preparing for teaching: observing, diagnosing, assessing and contextualising teaching material. But above all, enquiries allow the children to teach each other. When running the session 'Sentences', one eight-year-old girl called Briony created her own sentence: $\square$ = 'square' = 'a plain, closed figure with four equal sides connected by right angles', drawing in her own extra '=' sign to complete her sentence; when asked to explain her sentence she said that '=' means the same as 'the same as'. Given that many of the children will think that '=' means 'the answer', this is an essential bit of clarification that the class had been given. When faced with the following sum: '1+1+1', '+', '1', '=' '4' and its inverse: '4', '=', '1+1+1', '+' '1', most of them were unphased by the second of the two. And those that understood it could explain it very clearly to those that were struggling. In fact, because you have taken your foot off the teaching gas, as it were, it allows the space for the children to teach each other the very things you would probably have gone on to teach them anyway.

Links

See 'Web of understanding' in *The If Machine* for more on this method.

Iffing, anchoring and opening up

This combination of strategies helps to encourage structured thinking and expression, implicitly inviting the students to say whether what they said supports their view on the question. So, if the question is 'Can computers think?' then they will either be thinking 'yes', 'no', 'something else' such as 'yes *and* no' – see 'Carve it up!" on page 30 – or neither (for instance, if they don't understand the question). If they hold a positive, unqualified thesis (either 'yes' or 'no') then the question is turned into a statement: e.g. 'Yes, I think computers can think.' This is their conclusion. But children don't always say all of this; they might just say 'Thinking is just calculating.' By *iffing* this (see page 77) and by *anchoring* it (see page 7) to the main question: 'So, if thinking is just calculating, then can computers think?' the student is brought to decide (or recognise?) what conclusion this brings them to have (albeit provisionally e.g. 'Yes.' Then a simple opening up question (see Appendix 1) lets us into their reasons (or premises): 'Would you like to say why?', 'Because computers calculate, so …' The implicit argument here is:

- If computers calculate, then they can think (because calculating is thinking).
- Computers calculate.
- Therefore computers can think.

From a logical point of view, this also affords you a legitimate opportunity to introduce a possible controversy to the class – 'Is calculating the same as thinking?' (see 'Conceptual comparisons' on page 110) – because that 'calculating is just thinking' is an assumption that, according to the logical and sequential demands of a philosophical conversation, needs to be questioned. (See, in particular, 'Equipment and preparation needed' on page ix.)

DOING NOTHING

Thinking about doing and nothing

The most you'll ever have done doing nothing! And a perfect companion session to 'Thinking About Nothing' in The If Machine.

Equipment and preparation needed
- A whiteboard and pen
- A ball other than the talk-ball

Key controversies
Is it possible to do nothing? Can something without a will or the power of agency perform an action?

Possible misconception
That verbs are only 'doing' words and that being done to is the same as doing

Key concepts and vocabulary
Action	Doing	Intention
Agency	Event	Nothing
Anything	Force	Something
Being	Happening	Verb

Subject links
Literacy
Science
(forces)

Key facilitation tool
Break the circle on 'do'

KEY FACILITATION TOOL

Break the circle on 'do'

This is a basic conceptual analysis tool that encourages the children not to fall into circular definitions when explaining concepts. To use it, do as instructed, replacing 'do' with whatever word you want the children to analyse.

Say: I would like you to say what 'do' means but without saying the word 'do' or 'doing' in your answer. Begin by saying 'It is …' so you don't have to say 'Doing is … .'

Do:
1. Write 'It is …' at the top left-hand corner of the board.
2. Give the class a minute or two to talk with each other about what *doing* is.
3. Then write up their ideas as a concept-map (see page 88) in order to discuss the answers. If someone accidentally says 'do' or 'doing', ask them to think of another word or phrase they can say in place of the word 'do'. If they can't, ask someone else to help them.

Say: Today I have a task for you. The task is this: do nothing. Talk to each other in pairs to decide how you will attempt to do nothing. Then when I hold the ball in the air put up your hands if you think you can perform the task: to do nothing.

Do: Give the class a minute to think through how they might do nothing. Then remind them that they should be ready to show the class how to do nothing. Invite students to perform the task: to do nothing.

As with any task-based starter for philosophy, the model for this part of the discussion is to have someone 'do nothing', then to ask the class whether they think their classmate managed to do nothing or not. Repeat this pattern as many times as necessary; that means for as long as it takes to get the class involved in discussing the controversy that emerges when those that think you can do nothing engage with those that think you can't. Remember to use the imaginary disagreer strategy (see Appendix 1) if unanimity stands in the way of a good controversy.

THE DOING STATUE

Say: Everyone stand up and make a pose like a statue. Hold it and stay absolutely still for 20 seconds.

Task question: Do statues do anything?

Nested questions
- If statues stand and stare then are statues doing anything?
- Do statues stand? Do statues stare?
- If someone pushes a statue and makes it fall over has the statue done something?
  - What is it *to do* something?
  - What is doing?
  - What is a verb? Are verbs only 'doing words'?

Are the following words/phrases examples of doing something?
- Sitting
- Sleeping
- Being dead

The doing ball

Roll a ball to someone (X) in the class. Ask the following two questions:

- Did X [insert student's name] do something?
- Did the ball do something?

Present the (nicely structured) argument to the class:

Statues stand there,
'Stand' is a verb,
Verbs are doing words,
So, Statues do do something.

Then invite them to critically engage with it: 'Do you agree with this idea?' The girl's argument rests on a belief that verbs are *only* 'doing words' (see 'Possible misconception' above). This presents a good opportunity to teach the children that verbs are more than *doing* or *action* words.

Task question: **Is human will a force, like gravity?**

The doing robot

A robot is programmed to perform an act such as stealing something.

Task question: **1. Did the programmer do something?**

Task question: **2. Did the robot do something?**

Task question: **3. Who should be held responsible?**
(This adds a moral dimension to the discussions)

Nothing in a box

Task: find nothing!

Set the class the task of *finding* nothing and showing it to the class. If necessary you could explain that you've brought *nothing* in to the class today to show the children *nothing*. Take out an empty box and open it explaining that 'inside here is some *nothing*'. If necessary, follow this up with this question:

Task question: Have I managed to find nothing and show it to you?

Game: Statues

For a bit of fun to end with, have the entire class stand up and strike a pose like a statue. The aim of the game is to stay standing without moving or laughing for one minute. You should do some small things to try to distract them (though not too much!) such as pull a few faces, strike a funny pose or make a silly noise. If someone moves or laughs they are 'out' and should sit down. The winners are those still standing once one minute has elapsed.

Heidegger in the classroom

The German philosopher Martin Heidegger famously said, 'the nothing *noths*'.

Hermeneutic question: What do you think this might mean?

Task question: Does nothing itself do anything?

Links

Let's Do Nothing by Tony Facile

The If Machine: Thinking About Nothing; The Robbery

The Philosophy Shop: Dirty Deeds Done Dirt Cheap; Immy's Box; Lucky and Unlucky; Not Very Stationary Stationery; Ooops!; The Good Daleks

THE CEEBIE STORIES: THE THINKING TEST

Thinking about thinking

This session is an extension to the Ceebie stories in The If Machine but is also a stand-alone session. I would recommend using the opportunity to have the children turn their thoughts on their own thinking processes: how do they work things out? How do they know when they've done it?

Equipment and preparation needed
• A calculator

Key controversies
Is the ability to work something out the same as thinking? If correctly answering a sum proves that Ceebie can think, does the children's failing to correctly answer a sum prove that they can't think?

Subject links
Maths
Robots
Science
Testing hypotheses
(creating a fair test)

Possible misconception
That the appearance of thinking is sufficient for thinking

Key concepts and vocabulary
Computing   Understanding
Thinking   Working out

Key facilitation tool
Iffing, anchoring and opening up (see page 53)

In *The If Machine* classes are introduced to the characters of Ceebie, the computer-robot friend of a boy called Jack who struggles to make friends, and his human friend Tony. Ceebie and Jack have proved to be perennial favourites of many of the classes I've worked with. This is an extension activity to the second story, 'The Tony Test', and can be inserted into the longer narrative (just before it) or it can be used as a stand-alone session. It is not, however, simply a rewrite of 'The Tony Test', as this session covers different aspects of the same debate: 'Can computers think?' You may want to incorporate the first of the extension activities 'What about you?' into the session rather than waiting until afterwards.

Say: Jack is a boy who is shy and struggles to make friends. His dad is the owner of a factory that makes computer-robots, so he decides to build Jack a computer-robot friend, the CB1000, that Jack nicknames 'Ceebie'. When Jack introduces Ceebie to his new human friend, Tony, at first Tony refuses to believe that Ceebie can be a real friend. One reason he gives is that real friends need to be able to think and – so Tony argues – Ceebie can't think because he's just a computer-robot. Jack thinks that computer-robots might be able to think, so he proposes that they perform a test to find out, once and for all, whether Ceebie can think or not.

Task question: 1. Can you think of a test that would prove whether Ceebie can think or not?

Nested questions

- What is thinking?
- What is a test?
- How would you test for thinking?
- What (variables) would you need to consider when putting your test together?
- What would you need to be able to prove it?

Do: Allow the children to think about this is groups or pairs and then share some of the ideas. Ask the class to say whether they agree that the proposed tests prove that Ceebie can think. If you have already run 'The hypothesis box' (see page 90), you could frame this as a hypothesis:

Hypothesis: Computer-robots can think.

Task question: 2. What would you need to do to show that this hypothesis is true or false?

If necessary, and only to supplement their own suggestions, use the following example. The arguments below are based on arguments I often hear in classrooms; for this reason you may find that the children anticipate the arguments from Tony and Jack. I suggest that you 'do' the test with the class as you tell the story. For this you will need a calculator.

Say: Jack suggests that they could ask Ceebie a maths sum, and if Ceebie can answer it correctly it would prove that Ceebie can think. Tony agrees. Jack asks Ceebie, 'What does 12 + 10 equal?' Ceebie replies, without a pause, '22'. Tony and Jack work it out themselves and agree that Ceebie has answered the question correctly.

Do: Have the children think of a sum that is easy enough for them to be able to verify for themselves.

Task question: 3. Does this prove that Ceebie can think?

Say: Then Tony says that this doesn't prove whether Ceebie can think because the sum was too easy. 'It will only prove that Ceebie can think if he can answer a much more difficult sum,' says Tony. Then he asks Ceebie, 'What's 1000 minus 175?'

Without a pause Ceebie says, '825.'

Jack looks at Tony and says, 'Is that right? Coz I don't know?'

Tony looks puzzled and says, 'I don't know either. We'll have to work it out?'

Task question: 4. Is Ceebie right? How do you know?

Say: Once they have worked it out and found the answer to be correct Tony says, 'But it's still too easy for a computer. We need to think of the most difficult sum possible.'

Task question: 5. If Ceebie can correctly answer the most difficult sum Jack and Tony can think of, does that prove that Ceebie can think?

Nested questions

- When you work out the more difficult sum, does that prove that you can think?
- What is thinking?

EXTENSION ACTIVITY

What about you?

Do: You may want to have the class turn the enquiry back towards themselves. If so, make sure that you find out how they know the answers to the sums and how they worked it out. Ask them if their being able to work it out proves that they can think! You may notice how some will test the answers differently. Ask for a show of hands to these questions (and others you think of that are relevant):

- Hands up if you worked it out for yourself. (If so, ask them how. Also ask them how certain they are that the answer they worked out is right. How do they decide how certain they are?)
- Hands up if you 'know' because certain children in the class are good at arithmetic and they said they know.
- Hands up if you will only 'know' when you check it on a calculator. (Ask them how they will know whether the calculator has got it right?)
- Hands up if you will only 'know' if the teacher tells you the answer. (Ask them how they will know whether the teacher has got it right?)

THE DISAPPEARING BALL TRICK

Thinking about existence

This one employs a favourite device of mine: the disappointing, fake magic trick; I find it a galvaniser to good thinking. Two general questions behind this device are: 'Exactly why is this not an example of X?' and 'If this is not X, then what is X?' (See also 'Here's a Thought' on page 4 and 'The telekinetic teacher' on page 130).

Equipment and preparation needed
- A ball (other than the talk-ball)
- A glass of water with only a small amount of water in it
- Some Lego (or similar toy) pieces

Key controversies
Is it possible to make something no longer exist?
Is a thing the same as the parts it is made of?

Subject links
Science (dissolving, evaporation, diffusion)

Key concepts and vocabulary

Atoms	Object	The principle
Being	Parts	of the
Existence	Persistence	conservation
Identity		of energy

PART 1: A CHEAP TRICK!

Say: Today I am going to perform a really great magic trick. Are you ready? You'd better be, because it's going to be pretty amazing! I am going to make this ball [hold it up] no longer exist! Are you ready? Drum roll! [Put the ball behind your back.] Ta da!

Do: Allow them to respond and, if necessary, ask the following start-question: (Be careful not to change this to 'Have I made the ball disappear?' which is a very different question!)

Start question: Have I made the ball no longer exist?

PART 2: ANOTHER TRY

Say: OK, I'll try again. I will now proceed to make the ball no longer exist.

Do: Step out of the room, put the ball down on the floor outside, come back in and close the door.

Say: Ta da!

Do: Allow the class to respond and, if necessary, ask the start-question again.

Start question: Have I made the ball no longer exist?

Again, if necessary, move to the main task question:

Task question: How, if at all, would you be able to make the ball no longer exist?

Nested questions

- What is it for something to exist?
- Is it possible to make something no longer exist?
- Is something the same as its parts?
- Would the following ways make the ball no longer exist (all suggestions from classes):
  - Blowing it up?
  - Putting it somewhere where no one knows where it is?
  - Disintegrating it?
  - Putting the atoms it's made of in different parts of the universe?
- What does exist mean?

EXTENSION ACTIVITY

An activity with Lego

Do: Get hold of some Lego pieces (or a similar toy for constructing things) and ask one of the children to make a bowl or a pencil-holder with the pieces (in other words, something that can be *used as* the thing they have made). Fill the bowl or pencil holder so that it is being used as a bowl or pencil holder.

Task question: Is it a [insert item that it is]?

Nested questions

- Was it a [insert item] before you made it?
- If it is a [insert item], then when did it become one?
- If it is a [insert item], what makes it a [insert item]?
- If it isn't a [insert item], then what is it?
- If they had made a car, would it be a car?
- Is there a difference between a toy car and a pencil holder?

Do: Ask someone to take the item apart, piece by piece, until there's just a pile of pieces. Ask the following task question:

Task question: Have you made the [insert item] no longer exist?

Nested questions

- Is a thing the same as the parts it's made of?
- Are the parts the same as the thing they make?
- If it is no longer a [insert item], then where, if anywhere, did the [insert item] go?

Links

Once Upon an If: Water People; The Six Wise Men; The Patience of Trees; As Clear as the Edge of a Cloud

The If Machine: The Chair; Can You Step in the Same River Twice?; The Ship of Theseus; The Rebuild

The Philosophy Shop: A Knife Idea; A Heap of Exercises?; The Philosophical Adventures of Pencil Person; Backtracking; Not Half the Man He Used To Be

The Philosophy Foundation website: In another class (a lesson plan on 'vagueness').

A PLAN

Starting to think about business ethics

This is a good place to start thinking more deeply not only about business ethics but about goodness more generally and some of its different forms, such as moral goodness ('It's good not to lie'), prudential goodness ('It would be a good thing to take my umbrella') and instrumental goodness ('It would be good to invite him to my birthday, then he'll invite me to his').

Equipment and preparation needed
- Learn the story to tell (optional)
- A pair of scissors
- A whiteboard and pen

Key controversies
Was what the boy did morally wrong? Is good business-sense always moral? What is the relationship between business and justice?

Subject links
PSHE

Key facilitation tool
Is/Ought questioning (see page 71)

Key concepts and vocabulary
Business ethics
Calculation
Entrepreneurialism
Good (moral, instrumental, prudential)
Problem-solving
Risk

Do: Begin by reading or telling the following story. This story works well with some 'Instant dramatisation' (see page 154) to help with the class's understanding of the details of the story. (There are many Internet versions of this story. This is my own retelling.)

Say: *One day a boy bought a goat from a farmer for the equivalent of £50, but when the farmer came to deliver the goat he said to the boy that the goat had since died. The boy asked for his money back, but the farmer confessed that he had already spent the money so was unable to give it back.*

The boy thought for a minute and then said, 'OK, I'll take the goat anyway!' The farmer said, surprised, 'All right, if you're sure,' and quickly gave him the goat before the boy changed his mind.

A little while later the farmer passed the boy, who was now dressed in the finest clothes. 'You look wealthy!' the farmer said. 'What did you do with that dead goat I sold you?'

'I raffled it off for £2 a ticket,' the boy said, smiling.
'Didn't the people who bought the raffle tickets get angry with you when they found out that the goat was dead?' asked the farmer.
'No,' replied the boy, 'because the only person who found out was the winner. I simply apologised to him and said that, unfortunately, the goat had since died. Then I gave him back his £2 and another £10 for his trouble. He was more than happy with that.'
'So, how many tickets did you sell?' asked the farmer.
'Two hundred,' said the boy.
'Maybe if more of my goats died I'd be richer!' said the farmer.
'You need more than dead goats; you need a plan,' said the boy, then he left, counting his money.

Comprehension question: Can you explain the boy's plan and how it made him rich? (If necessary, use the board to help the class piece together the plan.)

Alternatively, you could try the following comprehension exercise:

1. Pair everyone up into an A and a B.
2. Have the As and the Bs turn to each other.
3. Give the As one or two minutes to say what happened in the story to their B partner.
4. Then have the Bs say anything they thought the A missed out or got wrong.

Task question: Was the boy's plan a good plan?

Nested questions

- What is meant by 'good'?
- Are there different meanings of 'good'? (For example *moral*, *prudential*, *instrumental* goods; see the 'Break the circle' activity on the opposite page for having the children draw their own distinctions.)
- Was what the boy did the right thing to do?
- If you were the winner, would you mind?
- If you were one of the losers, would you mind?
- If you were the farmer, would you mind?
- Did the boy do anything wrong?

Break the circle

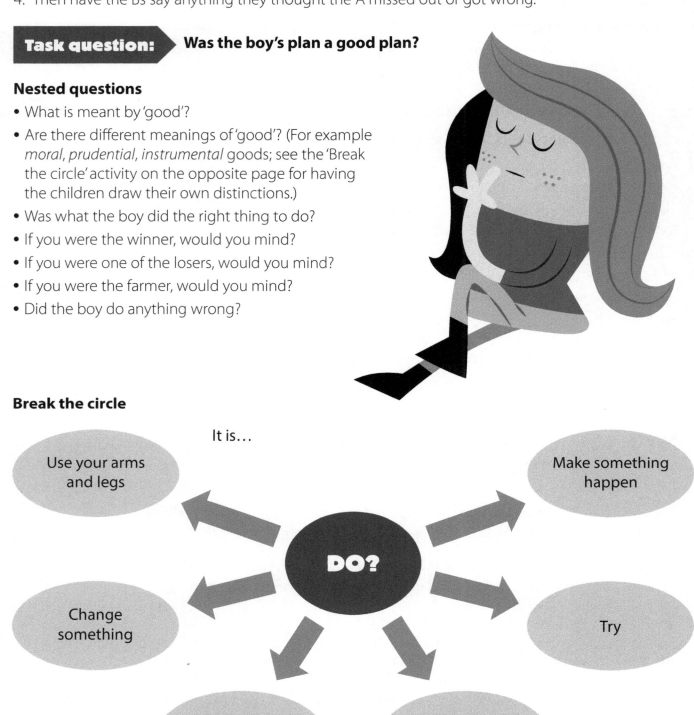

It is…

Use your arms and legs

Make something happen

DO?

Change something

Try

Move

Make your body move

Run 'Break the circle' (see page 54) on the concept good – get hold of a pair of scissors, and then ask the following three questions together to act as contrasts, making sure you write them up on the board to help the class keep track of them:

1. Are the scissors a *good* pair of scissors?

2. Is the boy's plan a *good* plan?

3. Is the boy a *good* person?

Nested questions

• Are all the 'good's in the three questions the same kind of *good*?

EXTENSION ACTIVITY

What would the boy say?

When the children answer question 3 you may want to let 'the boy' have an opportunity to respond to any challenges from the class. If so, ask the children if they want to respond on the boy's behalf (in other words, with role-play), allowing a dialogue between the class and the boy to take place. A different child may take the boy's role with each response, or it could be the same child.

Links

Once Upon an If: Il Duomo; The Fair Well; The Two Sindbads; The Valley of The Diamonds; The Saddle; Sheherazad's Handbook

The If Machine: Republic Island; The Ring of Gyges

The If Odyssey: The Horror of the Rocks

The Philosophy Shop: The Wicked Which; Phil and Soph and The Egg; Charlie's Choice; The Salesman

Thoughtings: Naughty-Land

TPF website: Republic Island – economics by Melina La Firenze

DOING PHILOSOPHY

Doing for thinking

These little exercises make excellent warm-ups. Once you get the idea behind them you should be able to make more of your own up. The idea is to contain, within the task or question, a conceptual conflict that needs unpacking, such as 'Can you see without sight?' (See Ian Gilbert's Little Book of Thunks *for plenty more questions and tasks of this sort).*

Equipment and preparation needed
- Random number generator (optional) – see below

Key facilitation tool
Show me! and Possibling (see page 70)

Subject links
Literacy
PSHE

Key controversies
Do concepts X and Y fit together?

Key concepts and vocabulary

Complete	Success
Doing	Task
Philosophy	Testing

The idea behind this section is to offer a slightly different way into philosophy other than the usual question (see 'Here's a thought' on page 4 for a list of the main 'starters' for philosophy). These could act as fun warm-ups, though they are likely to turn into full-blown enquiries of their own. Some will lead directly to other session plans and some stand alone. Most of these little 'tasks' contain a conceptual conflict (see 'Conceptual analysis', see page 110) that the class just need to clarify in order to solve the problem. For example, the task to 'make a deliberate mistake' contains a possible conflict between 'deliberate' and 'mistake'. Contained within the concept of a mistake is that it be *non-deliberate* (an accident, for example) so that the idea of a 'deliberate mistake' is nonsense. However, it is not easy, just by consulting the dictionary, to resolve this; highlighting the difference between *conceptual analysis* (see page 110) and dictionary definitions. To help the children with this see 'Atomic questioning' below (also see 'Who's right?' on page 72). Here are some examples of how children try to complete the tasks. One eight-year-old boy, called Indigo, approached the task, to do something you weren't going to do, in the negative: he simply stayed where he was and said, 'I was going to get up and show everyone how to do something I wasn't going to do, but now I'm not going to.' A girl called Sophie asked someone else in the class to tell her what to do; they said, 'sit down on the floor' and she did so. Brilliant! And the rest of the class had plenty to say.

Say: Today we are going to do philosophy slightly differently to usual. We are going to be doing our philosophy. I will set a task and then ask for a few volunteers to try to successfully complete the task. I will then invite the rest of the class to say whether they think the volunteers have managed it or not. Any volunteers?

- **Do something without choosing.** (See also 'Metaphysics: Freedom' in *The Philosophy Shop*)
- **Do something without moving.** (See also 'Doing nothing' on page 54 for a full, related session plan and 'Dirty Deeds Done Dirt Cheap' in *The Philosophy Shop*)
- **Do something you don't want to do.** (See also 'The diary' on page 84 for a full, related session plan and 'The Sirens' in *The If Odyssey* + online supplement)
- **Do something that changes the future.** (See 'The Time Machine' on page 112 for a full, related session plan and 'Metaphysics: Time' in *The Philosophy Shop*)
- **Do something impossible.** (See also 'Impossibling' and 'More Impossiblings' in Thoughtings and 'Dis-ingenious' in *The Philosophy Shop*)
- **Make a deliberate mistake.** (See also 'The Accidental Confession' in *The Philosophy Shop*)
- **Tickle yourself.** (See also 'The Ticklish Grump' in *The Philosophy Shop*)
- **Do something you weren't going to do.** (See also 'The Otherwise Machine' and 'What Zeus Does When He's Bored', both in *The Philosophy Shop*)
- **Hide something so that you can't find it.** (See also 'Trying to Forget and Not Bothering to Remember' in *The Philosophy Shop*)
- **Do something for no reason.** (See also 'What Goes Up …' in *The Philosophy Shop*)
- **Two of you must chase each other at the same time.** (See also 'Dizzy' in *The Philosophy Shop*.)
- **Do something without thinking about it.** (See also 'Thinking About Nothing' in *The If Machine*)

The task question for all of these 'tasks', and other tasks, in this book, is this:

Task question: **Did X [insert volunteer's name] succeed in completing the task: did X [insert task]? (For example, 'Did Indigo succeed in completing the task: did Indigo do something he wasn't going to do?')**

ATOMIC QUESTIONING

(See also 'Who's right?' on page 72.)

To help the class tackle the problems/controversies within each task, making sure the children address each of the salient concepts, split the question into the task's conceptual parts. For example, if the task is to 'make a deliberate mistake', anchor each contributor to the following atomic questions:

- Was X's attempt deliberate?
- Was X's attempt a mistake?

This strategy, what I call 'atomic questioning', can be used generally, and helps to break more complicated questions up into more manageable, bite-sized chunks, while making sure the children address each relevant conceptual component in their answer.

Links

See the list of tasks above.

Show me!

Closed questions elicit responses from children even before they've had a chance to properly think something through (see Appendix 1). This means that, for instance, very young children don't have to have a fully formulated answer before they are able to respond. Well, in some cases saying anything at all can be a problem, particularly with very young children (aged three to five), so here's another strategy: *you can ask children to show you*. This works particularly well when you have presented your stimulus with props (with teddy bears, for example), to 'dramatise' a scenario (see Berys and Morag Gaut's book *Philosophy For Young Children* for some wonderful examples of how to do this). If a child is struggling to explain an idea, or to get any words out at all, just point to the props and say, 'Can you show me?' Or, give them a whiteboard and a pen and say, 'Can you draw it for me?' Thanks to *The Philosophy Foundation*'s early-years specialist, Mr. Steve Hoggins for this very simple, yet helpful, tip.

Possibling

In my book *Thoughtings* there is a poem called 'Impossibling' (pages 74–77) that invites the reader to think of something impossible to do. *Possibling* is a related questioning strategy where you ask, 'Is it possible to do X?' (For example, 'Is it possible to do something you don't want to do?') This is a *leading question*, but I think, a *good kind* of leading question (not all leading questions are bad! It is not bad as long as you are open to suggestions that it either *is* or *is not* possible). Only use this strategy, however, once the children have begun to identify problems with performing the task – if they can't actually *perform* the task there and then but can *think* of a situation where it could be completed, such as hiding something from themselves. This strategy directly challenges the class to try to think of a way to complete the task, or to conclude that it is not possible.

Is/Ought questioning or, is-ing and ought-ing

If students give a *descriptive* answer to a moral or ethical question (what I call 'is-ing'), then follow this up with a *moral* formulation of the question (what I call 'ought-ing'), being careful not to *moralise* or use the dismissive 'but', but use 'and' or 'so' instead. So, if the question is 'Is it OK to hit someone back if they hit you?' and someone answers, 'Everyone does it' then your follow-up question could be: 'So, if everyone does it, does that mean that we *should* do it?' This is another example of a leading question, but as with the example in 'Doing philosophy' on page 68, I think it a justified use of a leading question because children are often not aware of the *is/ought distinction*, and because there is a necessary, logical relationship between the two sides of this ethical coin. It would be a *bad* leading question if you wanted the student to come to your view about it and used questions of this sort to achieve that. So, if the student concludes that the facts do bring us to a moral imperative, then it might just be that the student is an *ethical naturalist* (see below). If the class is old enough, there's no reason why you couldn't explain this distinction to them. Here's a good general, meta-ethical task question to accompany the *is/ ought questioning* strategy, around which a good enquiry can be had:

Task question: **If many/all people do X, does that mean that X is the right thing to do?**

Note: Try inserting a variety of different examples in place of X, such as (or ask the children to provide some examples, using these as back-up):

- Play/like football
- Be honest
- Lie
- Keep/Break promises
- Kill
- Not reveal all the faults of a house when trying to sell it (one for the teacher!)

Nested questions

- If only one person does X, is that a reason to do or not do X?
- Does the number of people who do X affect whether we should do X?
- Does the right thing have anything to do with what humans do?
- Do we think the same way about animals?
- Compare the following two examples:
  - Lions kill, therefore it is OK for lions to kill.
  - Humans kill, therefore it is OK for humans to kill.
- Now compare these two:
  - Lions have evolved to eat meat, so it is OK for lions to eat meat.
  - Humans have evolved to eat meat, so it is OK for humans to eat meat.
- In the above examples do the facts about lions or humans tell us anything about what lions and humans should do?
- The view that what we should do in some way derives from facts about us as a species is known as 'ethical naturalism'. Ethical naturalists think that the *is*, in some way at least, tells us what the *ought* is. For example, some humanists argue like so: 'humans have evolved to be social and moral, so humans *should* work towards a morally good social infrastructure.' (For those who think there are no grounds for moving from an *is* to an *ought*, this argument would have committed what's known as 'the naturalistic fallacy'.)

WHO'S RIGHT?

Thinking about disagreement

Does the received wisdom that everyone is entitled to their opinion mean that one's opinion can't be wrong? This session invites the class to tackle this controversy for themselves while providing you with some structure and strategies to help them do so.

Equipment and preparation needed
- Have the poem 'The Hodja's Royal Dinner' ready to project or hand out (optional)
- Have A4 scrap paper or whiteboards ready

Subject links
Literacy
Logic
PSHE

Key controversies
Can two people disagree and both be right?

Key concepts and vocabulary
Argument   Disagreement
Belief   Truth
Contradiction

Possible misconception
That an opinion cannot be wrong

Key facilitation tool
Atomic questioning and Opening up: exemplification

KEY FACILITATION TOOL

Atomic questioning

This is when you take a question that has more than one relevant conceptual component and turn it into more than one question to make sure that the children have addressed each component. So, in the example below, the question 'Can two people disagree and both be right?' can be broken into two more 'atomic' questions: 1. 'In your example, are they both right?' and then, 2. 'Is it a disagreement?' (See 'Doing philosophy' on page 68 for another example of this strategy.)

INTRODUCTION TO THE HODJA

Say: The Hodja is a story character thought to have originated from Turkey, though he and his stories are found in many other cultures around the world. The Hodja – also known as Nasreddin, Mulla Nasreddin or Efendi – is sometimes wise and sometimes a fool, sometimes unemployed and sometimes a judge or religious leader. His stories are often humorous, puzzling and thought-provoking. Many of them are very short, barely qualifying as stories at all.

Do: Read or tell the following story to the class.

Say: The Hodja has gone up in the world and in this story he is acting as a qadi – a judge. Today, he is to listen to a case in which there is a disagreement between two neighbours. The first of the neighbours stands before him and explains his side of the story to the Hodja. The Hodja listens attentively for ten minutes or so. Once the man has finished the Hodja considers for a minute and then says, 'You are right!' Next, the second of the two neighbours stands before him and explains his side of the story. Again, the Hodja listens and, again, he considers and then says, 'You are right!' Now, the Hodja's wife has been listening to everything. When she hears what the Hodja says to the second neighbour, she stands up and says, 'Hodja! They can't both be right!' The Hodja thinks for a moment and then says to his wife: 'You are right!'

Task question: So, who is right?

Nested questions

- Are there any disagreements two people can have where both people can be right?
- Are there any disagreements two people can have where only one of them can be right?
- What makes something right and what makes something wrong?
- Is being right and wrong just a matter of opinion?
- Can everyone be right?
- What is an opinion?
- What is a fact?

KEY FACILITATION TOOL

Opening up: exemplification

Because of the abstract nature of this story (there's no content to the disagreement) remember to open up the students' points with *exemplification opening up* questions (see 'closed questions' in Appendix 1): 'Can you give an example?'

To help the class with the difficult logic of this story I write the following up on the board and have the class fill it in as I write (by shouting out):

1. H to N1 = 'You're right!'
2. H to N2 = 'You're right!'
3. W to H = 'They can't both be right!'
4. H to W = 'You're right!'

Task question: If the Hodja's wife is right, can both of the neighbours be right?

Filling in the story

Say: So far, we don't actually know what the two neighbours disagreed about. So, can you think of any examples where two people disagree with each other but where they are both right? You may think that it's impossible, but let's see if we can think of any examples first.

Do: Give the class talk-time to think of some examples.

Use *anchoring* (see page 7) and *atomic questioning* (see page 72) here. Anchor all the children that offer examples to the following two questions:

1. Is [the example] a disagreement?
2. Are they both right?

For the example to be successful one needs to be able to answer 'yes' to both questions. Invite the whole class to respond, not just those that offered the example. Write any examples up on the board, or on two A4-sized whiteboards, next to each other, like so:

 My favourite colour is red.   *My favourite colour is blue.*

Here are some examples that I've heard:

- 'Me and my friend, when we were little, were arguing. I said, 'I'm taller than you,' and she said, 'No, I'm shorter than you.' These two girls, in the end, decided that they *were* both right but that it wasn't really a disagreement, as they only *thought* they disagreed. Sounds like a correct analysis to me.
- 'Cats are lovely.'/'Cats are horrible.'

Here are some examples you can try out with the class if necessary, and remember to anchor the children back to questions 1 and 2 above:

- 'My favourite colour is red.'/'My favourite colour is blue.'
- 'The best colour is red.'/'The best colour is blue.'
- '2 + 2 = 4'/'2 + 2 = 5'
- 'It is my opinion that 2 + 2 = 4'/'It is my opinion that 2 + 2 = 5'

Some children analyse the problem by saying that 'Neither of them is right' or 'They can't be right'.

Content version

Here's my verse version of another Hodja story that provides some content for the structure in the first Hodja story.

The Hodja's Royal Dinner

The Hodja had been invited to dine
With the King and Queen,
No less.

The food was said to be very fine,
The best ever been,
No less.

The King declared the soup the best –
The Hodja heartily agreed,
But the Queen said, 'No, the lamb's the finest dish' –
And the Hodja heartily agreed!

The Queen reminded Nasreddin,
'Saying "yes" to both makes no sense;
Just now you agreed with the royal King.'
To which the Hodja made this defence:

'I serve my King and I serve my Queen;
Not the soup or lamb tagine!'

Task question: ▶ **So, has the Hodja provided us with an example where two people disagree but where they are both right?**

The Bridge of Death

Do: To show the scene follow this link: https://goo.gl/lBLYp8

Say: In the film *Monty Python and the Holy Grail* there is a scene in which King Arthur and his remaining knights, on their quest for the Holy Grail, come to a bridge that crosses 'the Gorge of Eternal Peril'. There is a bridge keeper who bars the way across the bridge. When the first knight, Sir Lancelot, approaches the 'bridge of death' the bridge keeper says, 'Who would cross the bridge of death must answer me these questions three, ere the other side he see.' He is asked three simple questions: 'What is your name?', 'What is your quest?' and 'What is your favourite colour?' Sir Lancelot answers the questions easily and is allowed to cross the bridge. This is what happens when Sir Galahad is asked the three questions:

Bridge Keeper: Stop! What is your name?
Sir Galahad: Sir Galahad of Camelot.
Bridge Keeper: What is your quest?
Sir Galahad: I seek the Grail.
Bridge Keeper: What is your favourite colour?
Sir Galahad: Blue. No, yel— Agggggghhhhhh!! [He is cast into the Gorge of Eternal Peril]

Task question: **Is it possible to be wrong about something like your favourite colour?**

Nested questions

- How can you be wrong about a preference such as your favourite colour?
- Could you be insincere and say a colour is your favourite colour when it's not because of who you are with? In this case, would it be right to say that you are wrong about your favourite colour?
- Is it possible to be wrong about your favourite colour even if you are sincere?
- Is it possible to not know what your favourite colour is?
- If you don't know what your favourite colour is then can you be wrong about it?
- Can something like your favourite colour change?
- If it can, does that mean that you can be wrong about your favourite colour?

Links

Once Upon an If: The Cat that Barked; The Six Wise Men; Flat Earth; The Fire Stick
Provocations by David Birch: Facts and Opinions (though a book for secondary schools, this is a session that works well with older primary children)
The If Machine: The Shadow of the Pyramid
The If Odyssey: Captain or Crew?; Clouded
The Philosophy Shop: Green Ideas; Said and Unsaid; Tralse; Dizzy; Phil and Soph and the Numbers; Some Sums With Zero

RULERS

Thinking about knowledge and stealing

Inspired by Michael Hand's entry for **The Philosophy Shop** *'The Pencil'*
this session uses an everyday and seemingly uncontroversial starting
place to allow the children to apply some reasonable doubt to think about
knowledge, stealing and the relationship between the two.

Equipment and preparation needed

- A standard classroom ruler
- A less standard, more unique-looking item

Subject links

PSHE
All knowledge-based subjects

Key controversies

When are you able to say that you know something? Are all cases of taking other people's things stealing? What role does knowing play in stealing?

Possible misconception

That thinking you know something is the same as knowing something

Key concepts and vocabulary

Borrow	Ownership
Find	Permission
Intention	Property
Know	Steal

Key facilitation tool

Iffing (see below)

KEY FACILITATION TOOL

Questioning strategy: iffing

This enquiry is great for seeing how the questioning strategy *iffing* (see 'Iffing' on page 36) works. Imagine that you were to come back into the classroom holding the ruler in the other hand, and one of the children were to say, 'It's not the same ruler because you came back in holding it in the *other* hand.' Given that it is possible you don't even remember doing it, the simplest way to deal with this is to say (to the whole class and not just the speaker): 'If I came back into the class holding the ruler in a different hand, would that mean that it is a different ruler or not?' Iffing can also be used with the children's response to the narratives. If someone says something like, 'But maybe he knows it's Jenny's, maybe he's seen her use it,' then 'if' it both ways (see Either-or-the-if on page 111): 'If he does know that it's Jenny's then would he be stealing it if he takes it?' Take a response then say, 'And if he doesn't know it's Jenny's but just sees a ruler, then would he be stealing it if he takes it?'

Do: Take a standard ruler or similar object, of which you have many in the school, making sure that it has no distinguishing features.

Say: I have with me a ruler, as you can see.

Do: Step out of the room for a short period of time, taking the ruler with you, then go into the classroom.

Task question: 1. Is this the same ruler?

Task question: 2. Do you *know* that it is the same ruler?

Nested questions
- If so, then how do you know?
- What is knowing?
- How do you know something?
- How do you know that you know something?
- Is there a difference between 'thinking you know something' and just 'knowing something'?

SCENARIO 1

Do: Narrate the following scenario (like the narrator in *Peppa Pig*!) to the class and have the scene dramatised, either by some other staff members or by some children (see 'Instant dramatisation' on page 153). Give the actor who is about to play 'Jenny' a ruler.

Say: Jenny has her ruler. She is very happy with her ruler. It is her favourite ruler. At some point in the day she loses it. Jenny is very upset to have lost her ruler. She goes to class upset that she has lost her ruler.

[*Exit* Jenny, leaving the ruler on the floor, 'lost'.]

Say: A little while later Sam comes along. He is annoyed because he forgot his ruler today. He is on his way to class and so needs a ruler to work with. Then, on the ground in front of him, he sees the ruler. 'Perfect! Just what I need,' he thinks to himself. Sam picks up the ruler and takes it to class with him, happy that he now has a ruler for the day. It's a nice one, too!

Task question: Did Sam steal Jenny's ruler?

Nested questions
- What is stealing?
- Does knowing play a role in answering this task question? If so, what role does it play?
- Can you steal something by accident?

Scenario 2

- You could repeat the scenario, the second time replacing the ruler with something less standard and more unique-looking.
- You could point out that the 'standard' rulers are school property and then return to the task question: Did Sam steal Jenny's ruler?

General application

The opening stimulus (walking out of the room with a ruler and then walking back in again) has a wider application: you could use this stimulus with any object where you want the children to think about *identity*, or whether one or two things are the same thing. You could even ask one of the children to step out of the classroom (or do so yourself) and then step back in again, asking: 'Is [insert name of person] the same person?'

Using the = sign

Another way to discuss identity in a way that all ages – including nursery – can join in with, is to ask if two things are the same. You could write two words up on the board with an equals sign in between them, and a question mark after. For example, 'mind = brain ?' Or, you could laminate two pieces of paper or card, one with '=' on and the other with '?' on, then simply place items (such as water and ice) in the appropriate place, or write words on A4 paper or whiteboards. The idea is for the children to understand (and use) the '=' sign to mean 'identical', not 'the answer'. Try these (see also 'Sentences' on page 47 and The dog that meowed on page 30):

- Odysseus = Ulysses ?
- Square = ☐ ?
- 2 = 2 ?
- 4 = 2 + 2 ?
- Same = similar ?

Links

Once Upon an If: The Six Wise Men; Flat Earth; Honest Sa'id; The Island

The If Machine: The Robbery

The Philosophy Shop: The Pencil; Not Very Stationary Stationery ('Rulers' can be thought of as an extension to Michael Hand's and A.C. Grayling's contributions. Try dramatising Michael and Anthony's sessions); The Adventures of Poppy the Bear; Knowing Stuff; Little Thea's Tricky Questions

Thoughtings: How do you know that?

THE TALKING SKULL

Thinking about evaluating claims

This great, traditional story brings the children to think about extraordinary claims (that includes miracles), whether they should be taken seriously, and if so, under what conditions. Heads will roll!

Equipment and preparation needed

- Something to stand in for the skull and Enitan's head, such as two balls (optional) – in addition to the talk-ball
- Have the *Thoughting* 'Talking is like …' ready to project or hand out (optional)
- A whiteboard and pen

Subject links

Literacy
PSHE
RE
Science

Key controversies

Should we believe people's accounts of miraculous events? Is talking a good thing?

Key concepts and vocabulary

Belief	Miracles
Communicate	Reasons
Communication	Talk
Knowledge	Tell
Magic	

Key facilitation tool

Quotes. Discuss.

KEY FACILITATION TOOL

Quotes. Discuss.

Statements can be very effective catalysts to thought, sometimes more effective than a question, as they can provoke a visceral response. Compare these two ways of putting an issue to someone: a. 'Are girls or boys better at writing?' b. 'Girls are better than boys at writing.' (See 'Provoke' on page 145.) One way to engage students is to put a quote to the class. It follows the exam question model where a statement is made followed by the word 'Discuss.' It is also one way to engage students with the wider community of thinkers. In the online resources that accompany this book you will find a list of statements and quotes to use with your students in this way.

DO: Read or tell the following story. It is only a little more than a synopsis, so feel free to embellish the story in your retelling, if you choose to tell it.

Say: *A long time ago, somewhere in Africa, there was once an honest, sensible man, called Enitan. One day, while walking through the jungle by himself, he found a human skull lying on the ground. He wondered how the skull had come to be there so he said, out loud to the skull, 'How did you get here?', not expecting an answer.*

'Talking brought me here,' said the skull. Amazed and terrified at what he had just witnessed, Enitan ran the rest of the way home.

He went to see the village chief and told him about the talking skull he'd found in the jungle, thinking that this would make him famous in the village.

Task question: **Should the village chief believe Enitan?**

Nested questions

- The man's story is extraordinary, so should the chief believe him?
- If the story is true, then should the chief believe him?
- Is it a miracle?
- What is a miracle?
- Could there be any other explanations for the skull talking?
- If someone tells you something unbelievable, should you believe him or her?
- If so, under what circumstances should you believe an unbelievable account?

Say: *The chief did not believe him. 'But I DID see a talking skull! I did! I DID!' Enitan protested.*

'OK,' said the chief, 'I, and two of my guards, will go with you; if the skull speaks I will reward you with treasures and fame, but if it does not … then I shall reward you with death.'

The chief, his guards and Enitan returned to the place where he had found the skull. Enitan bent down and said to the skull, 'How did you get here?' The skull said … nothing.

'HOW DID YOU GET HERE?' said Enitan again, louder this time. Still the skull remained silent. The king turned to his guards and said, 'This man has also wasted my time! Kill him!' So they chopped off his head, which fell to the ground next to the skull with a thud. The king and his guards returned to their village. Once they had departed, the skull opened its grinning mouth and said to Enitan's head, 'How did you get here?' and Enitan's head replied, 'Talking brought me here.'

Do: At this point you could do or adapt the PaRDeS method (see Appendix 2) with your class, especially if you think that many of the children have not fully understood the story; and/or you could ask the following task questions.

Comprehension question: Why did Enitan's head reply, 'Talking brought me here'?

Task question: Is talking a good thing?

Nested questions

- What is talking?
- What does talking help us achieve?
- What would we lose if we lost the ability to talk?
- What would the world be like without talking? (see 'The hiding box' on page 158)
- When and how might talking be bad?

Say: No one noticed: not Enitan, the chief or his guards, but lying in or on the ground, littered all over the place, were many more human skulls!

Comprehension question: Why are there lots of skulls?

EXTENSION ACTIVITY

Communicate something without talking

1. Have someone leave the room.
2. Identify an item in the room to another child.
3. Set the second child the task of communicating something – anything – about the item but without talking or using words *in any way*.

Questions:

- Can they do it?
- How easy is it?
- What methods did they use?

'Talking is like …' – a simile exercise

Do:

1. Go round the circle and say 'Talking is like …' to each child.
2. Give them three seconds to say a word without repeating another child's suggestion (employing 'the different answer rule' – see 'Facilitating idea-diversity' on Appendix 1).
3. Gather the words on the board as you go around.
4. Once everyone has had a go, ask all the children to *challenge* the words: for example, 'I don't understand how talking can be like X …'
5. Ask the class, as a whole, to respond and attempt to explain why talking is like X.

Here is a *Thoughting* based on the exercise that could be used in a similar way: ask the children to challenge the words in the *Thoughting* and have the class respond in its defence. If the children struggle to grasp the simile/metaphor essence of the task you could read the *Thoughting* first, in order to give them a flavour of the task, and then run the activity, stipulating that they should not repeat anything from the poem.

> ### Talking is like …
>
> A tool,
> An instrument,
> A cloak,
> A weapon,
>
> A map,
> A metal detector,
> Medicine,
> Poison.
>
> A virus,
> A wireless
> Kind of
> Connection.
>
> A finger
> That points
> To the farthest
> Location.
>
> With talk
> I walk
> But do not
> Move.
>
> With talk
> My thought-
> Hawk flies
> To you.

Talk-ball

Play a version of the BBC Radio 4 game *Just a Minute!* (Here called 'Talk-ball' because a minute is too long.) This is when a player has to speak on a subject, while holding the talk-ball, for a set time period without *hesitation*, *repetition* or *deviation*. I begin with a ten-second time period, then, when someone succeeds, extend the time to 15 seconds, then 20 seconds, and so on. The class choose up to eight topics, but the topic each speaker has to speak about is chosen randomly (see 'Random number generator' on page 101).

Links

Once Upon an If: Sheherazad's Handbook; The Cat that Barked

The If Odyssey: Nobody's Home (The Cyclops) – especially the online supplement 'Through a Philosopher's Eye: Cyclops'. In some versions of the Greek myth of the Trojan War, the character of Palamedes meets an ironic, tragic end when, he – the so-called inventor of writing – is undone by a written letter. In revenge for Palamedes' uncovering of Odysseus' attempt to escape being sent to Troy, Odysseus fakes a letter from Palamedes to Priam. Palamedes is stoned to death by Odysseus.

The Philosophy Shop: The Txt Book

THE DIARY

Thinking about willpower

This session provides an enquiry and some fun activities to have the children think through what the ancient Greeks called sophrosyne aka willpower, self-discipline, self-control. This makes an excellent follow-on session to 'The Singing Women (The Sirens)' in The If Odyssey.

Equipment and preparation needed

- A clock or timer
- Have the children seated in the talk-circle
- A book functioning as a diary (optional)
- A small object that you can easily keep in your pocket; anything you happen to have in your pocket will do, such as a phone

Key controversies

Is it possible to exercise power over your own will? Do you necessarily want to do whatever you do? Is it possible to do something you don't want to do, or, by doing it have you demonstrated your desire to do it? Can you want what you want whenever you want?

Key concepts and vocabulary

Desire
Self-control
Want
Want to want (second-order desire)
Willpower

Subject links

PSHE

Key facilitation tool

Concept-maps as tension detectors (see page 88)

Do: Begin by reading the following scenario to the class.

Say: Your best friend visits you and asks you to look after their personal diary for one week because they are going away and they don't want anyone to read it. You are asked not to read it yourself. 'Do you promise?' your friend asks.

Task question: Will you take the diary and will you promise not to read it?

Nested questions

- What *should* you say and what *should* you do?
- Is it possible to know what *you* would do in a similar situation?
- Is it a promise you should make?

You may want to make use of the following extension to the scenario at an appropriate moment during the discussion.

Say: A week later your friend comes to your house and asks, 'Did you read it?'

You say: 'No.'

'Have you got it?' they ask.

'No,' you say.

'Where is it then?' they ask.

You say: 'I burned it.'

'Why did you burn it?' they ask.

'So that I wouldn't read it,' you explain.

Task question: **Were you right to burn it?**

Nested questions

- Was burning it an act of willpower?
- If it was a choice between burning it and reading it, which would be the best thing to choose?
- Might there have been another option?

Do: At some point introduce the concept of *willpower* with the following three questions:

- What is willpower? Do a concept-map (see page 88) around this question.
- Do you need willpower in this situation?
- How would you use your willpower in this situation?

Anchor the children to the following question: 'Is X [whatever they have suggested, e.g. *burning the diary*] an example of willpower?

For the following exercises, have your timer ready or make sure you can easily see a clock.

WILLPOWER EXERCISE 1: THE TURN-AROUND TEST

Do: Use these exercises as discussion points about how easy or hard they were to resist taking part in. Use the questions in 'Key controversies' as possible task questions for enquiries around the exercises.

Say: I am going to set you a series of exercises in willpower. Remember: the overall task of these exercises is to demonstrate your own willpower; your own self-control. First of all everyone must stand up. Now turn around so that you are facing the walls of the classroom with your backs to me. The exercise begins when I count to three, at which point you must not turn around for a full ten seconds. If you do, you will not have completed the task. I will tell you when ten seconds has elapsed. One, two, three!

WILLPOWER EXERCISE 2: THE ORPHEUS TEST

Say: We are going to repeat the exercise, but with a few differences. Can everyone please stand up and turn around again. This time, the time will extend to 20 seconds and I am going to place a 'very interesting object' on the floor behind you. I will place the object on the floor as I say 'three' and will pick it up again when the 20 seconds has elapsed so you will not get to see the 'very interesting object'. One, two, three!

Do: When the children have turned around place your 'pocket object' (see 'Equipment and preparation needed') – any object – on the floor in the middle of the talk-circle. You may want to make the task harder for them … so, as the 20 seconds draws to a close you could say, 'It is a very interesting object that you won't get to see …' or count down: 'five, four, three, two …' Just before you say 'one' put the object back in your pocket. The following could make a good discussion point:

Task question: Given that these are exercises in willpower, was it fair of me to make it more difficult?

WILLPOWER EXERCISE 3: THE TOUCH-THE-GROUND-TURN-AROUND-AND-SIT-ON-YOUR-CHAIR TEST

Say: Before I tell you what the next exercise in willpower will be, you must not do anything until I count to three. This time there will be a competition. The winner will be the first person, once I count to three to [demonstrate as you read] touch the floor in front of them with their hand, to turn all the way around and then to sit on their chair. That person will be the winner of the game. However, that is not the task that you must complete. The task is not to compete in the game but to stay perfectly still. Once I have counted to three I will give you about ten seconds to stop yourselves competing. But remember: the winner is the first one to touch the ground, turn around and sit down. One, two, three!

WILLPOWER EXERCISE 4: THE QUESTION TEST

Say: For this exercise I am going to ask you a series of questions. The winner of the game is the first person to answer a question correctly. However, as before, that is not the task you are being set. The task, as before, is not to answer the questions – not to compete in the game – for the duration of this exercise.

Suggested questions:
- What is 30 minus 8?
- What is 2 squared?
- What is the capital of France?
- What is the sixth letter of the alphabet?

WILLPOWER EXERCISE 5: DON'T LAUGH!

Say: For this exercise everyone will need to stand up. The task this time is to remain standing up and silent for one minute without laughing. If you laugh, you must sit down. If you sit down then you will not have completed the task. If you are still standing at the end then you will have competed the task. Starting now!

Do: Again, to make this harder you could perform a few silly movements or pull a silly face or two (see note for Exercise 2: The Orpheus test).

EXTENSION ACTIVITY

More extension activites

- You could have members of the class dramatise the diary scenario to act as a stimulus (see 'Instant dramatisation' on page 153).
- Tell (or read) the story of Orpheus in The Underworld. Then do PaRDeS (see Appendix 2).
- Play some inhibitory control games such as 'Bippity-bippity-bop', 'Clap-jump-stop-go' (see the TPF website) and 'Simon says'.
- Show or explain 'The Stanford marshmallow experiment' (easily found online). If you introduce this at any point during the session, you need to be careful of one thing: the findings showed that those children who failed to resist did less well in life subsequently. However, this is a statistical conclusion, so it does not follow that if someone fails in one of the tests that they will do less well in life. It may be worth communicating this to the class if you explain the findings of the research.

Links

Frog and Toad Stories: 'The Cookies' by Arnold Lobel

Once Upon an If: The Old Man of The Sea

Related stories: The Story of Lot's Wife (from the Bible), Orpheus in The Underworld (see online)

The If Machine: Billy Bash; The Scorpion and the Frog; The Ring of Gyges

The If Odyssey: The Singing Women

The Philosophy Shop: Trying to Forget and Not Bothering to Remember; Arete and Deon; The Wicked Which

Thoughtings: Bite, It Wasn't Me!; The Wicked Which

Concept-maps as tension detectors

Concept-maps (a 'boarding' device where you note just key concept-words on the board, linking them with lines and/or arrows to show relationships) are good to help a class (and you!) keep track of where the discussion has been. In 'Using contradictions' on page 15, I suggest that contradictions and tensions can be a great learning tool; well, the concept-map is a great tool for bringing out tensions and contradictions. However, I've seen concept-maps not used to their full potential in the classroom, where they are used merely to list all the children's different ideas about a concept. This is the right way to start, but to use concept-maps to go further, they should be used to have the children see and then critically engage with each other over tensions that emerge from the listing part of concept-mapping. For example, the central concept might be 'mind'. One of the children says, 'Your mind is really your brain,' and the facilitator writes: 'mind = brain' coming off the central word (which is 'mind'). Someone else says, 'the mind is not physical, it's not *there*'. The facilitator writes, 'not physical', steps back and takes a look at what's on the board, then says to the first child, 'Is the brain physical?' and he says, 'Yes.' The facilitator then draws a 'two-direction' arrow between these two ideas with a big question mark in the middle and says, 'Is the mind physical?' to the whole class. This gets written up as an emergent task question and the children go to talk-time.

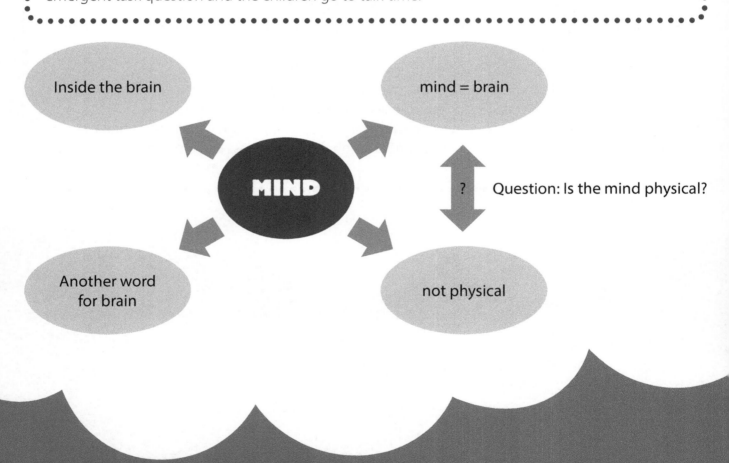

Experience as stimulus

Immersive experience can be a very powerful tool for engaging students. Storytelling, when done well, is immersive, and storytelling in the second person (see 'The hiding box' on page 156 for an example of this) is another level of immersive storytelling. In this session (The Never-Ending Letter, page 98), it is taken even further because the actual experience in the classroom becomes part of the story, with a little help from some drama. Grace Robinson of *Thinking Space* (www.thinkingspace.org.uk) and Jesse Walsh in the United States (Boston, MA) have some superb ways of making use of immersive drama and experiences to bring children to philosophical thinking. For instance, talking about discrimination is one thing, but Walsh has an activity (her philosophical game 'Hangwoman') in which one of the groups taking part is actively discriminated against. See the resources section at www.philosophy-foundation.org for Jesse Walsh's resources.

Carve it up!

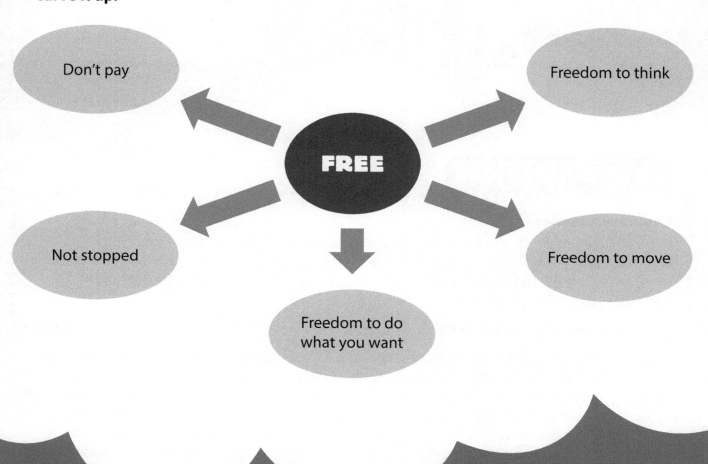

THE HYPOTHESIS BOX

Thinking about science

The main aim of this session is to explore the conditions necessary for showing a hypothesis to be true. No tests are performed and no experiments are constructed other than in the minds of the students. It is a reasoning exercise about what outcomes would be expected when X or Y is done and about what outcomes would show the hypothesis to be true.

Equipment and preparation needed
- An enclosed non-transparent box
- A ball (optional; see below)

Key controversies
How is philosophy related to science? Can religious belief be treated in a similar way to scientific belief or are the two realms of belief disanalagous?

Subject links
Philosophy
RE
Science

Key facilitation tool
Counter-examples

Key concepts and vocabulary

Demonstrate	Show
False	Test
Hypothesis	True
Knowledge	

KEY FACILITATION TOOL

Counter-examples

When children make claims, especially general claims, a good thing to have the class do is search for a counter-example to the claim. For instance, if someone says, 'Everything is possible' then, if the class has not already begun to do so, ask, 'Can anyone think of an example of something that is *not* possible?'

This kind of enquiry would be an excellent way to get a class to prepare for constructing tests and experiments in science and to consider what variables matter in relation to the hypothesis. This exercise also shows the links between science and philosophy – philosophy being reason-based and science being distinguished by being experimental and empirical as well as reason-based. You can see the close link in the example that follows because in thinking about the necessary conditions one needs to have a clear understanding of the concept 'object'. This is where the *conceptual analysis* aspect of philosophy has a clear and important role in scientific reasoning.

PART ONE: THE OBJECT HYPOTHESIS

DO: Before the session, and while the children are not there to see, put an item such as a ball in a box. Ask the class if anyone knows what a hypothesis is. Write up the word 'hypothesis' and do a concept-map around it (see 'Concept-maps as tension detectors' on page 88). Once this is done, provide the class with a definition. Here is the dictionary definition:

 … a supposition or proposed explanation made on the basis of limited evidence as a starting point for further investigation. Longman

Etymology: 'Hypothesis' comes from the ancient Greek for 'foundation' and later went on to mean 'to suppose'.

For a younger class, here's a simpler definition:

 A hypothesis is when you suppose something to be true before you know whether it is or not, so that you can test it to see if it's true.

Write the following hypothesis up on the board:

Hypothesis: *There is an object in the box.*

Task question: **How can we find out whether the hypothesis is true or false?**

Someone is likely to say, 'Open it.' If they do, this is how to respond (the structure of your questioning should follow – more or less – the lines of this example throughout this session):

Facilitator: If you open the box, then what (outcomes) would you expect? (*Eliciting expectations*)

Student: You might see an object or you might not.

Facilitator: If you open it and you see an object then have you shown the hypothesis to be true or false? (*Iffing and anchoring*)

Student: True.

Facilitator: Can you say why? (*Opening up – justification*)

Student: Because if there's something there then … [the student continues]

Facilitator: If you open it and you don't see an object in it, then have you shown the hypothesis to be true or false? (*Either-or-the-if and anchoring* - see page 111)

Student: That depends.

Facilitator: What would it depend on? (*Opening up – condition* – see 'Facilitating idea-diversity' on Appendix 1)

Student: What an *object* is. Because if a germ or bacteria is an object then it would be true, but if we mean something like …

The questioning strategies at the heart of this session are *iffing*, *anchoring* and *opening up* (see page 53) and – a new strategy – *eliciting expectations*. This is where you ask the student to say what outcomes they would need in order to show that what they are saying is true or, to put it as you will say it in this session, *to show the hypothesis to be true*. It is asking them to say what conditions are needed. In normal English, something like: 'So what do you need to be able to show that?'

THE UN-OPENABLE BOX

You could make this task harder by making the following stipulation: 'If you could not open the box (for whatever reason), then how would you be able to find out if the hypothesis is true?'

• Shake the box

• Weigh the box

• X-ray … and so on …

After each of these, or other, suggestions follow a similar structure to the 'object hypothesis' example above:

1. If you shake the box, what would you expect?

2. If something rattles inside, would you have shown the hypothesis to be true or false?

3. If something does not rattle inside then would you have shown the hypothesis to be true or false? And so on …

EXTENSION ACTIVITY

More hypotheses suggestions

Say: Here are some suggestions:

• There is a pineapple in the box. (If the box is too small for a pineapple then they are invited to think about whether there are any reasons that can be offered for the hypothesis's falsity without having to open the box. In other words, what philosophers call, an a priori reason: a reason so strong no evidence is needed.)

• All birds fly.

• Teddy bears come alive when no one is watching.

• CO_2 is the same as air.

• Water and ice weigh the same.

• Unicorns exist.

• The theory of abiogenesis is true (research 'abiogenesis' or the theory of 'spontaneous generation', associated with Aristotle, and also research Francesco Redi's famous experiments (1668) to test this hypothesis. Interestingly, the jury's still out on abiogenesis when it comes to the origins of life itself!)

Do: Do not perform the test or touch the box; explore, using the above questioning structure, *how* the children would test the hypothesis. As a science follow-up, you could try to perform the test that was thought up in the session.

OPEN THE BOX?

You may decide, at the end of the session, to open the box and reveal what is inside. However, there is another enquiry opportunity here about the nature and relationship of philosophy to science: you could ask the following two-part question:

- If this is a philosophy session then do we need to – and should we – open the box?
- If this were a science session would we need to – and should we – open the box?

Nested questions

- What are the similarities, if any, between philosophy and science?
- What are the differences, if any, between philosophy and science?

The students' responses to these can reveal two things: their understanding of the subjects of philosophy and science, and also their intellectual/philosophical maturity (see the children's response to 'The maybe cat' session on page 38). There may be those in the class who are sensitive to the intellectual value of not revealing what is inside the box. Those that respond in this way demonstrate, in my view, a sophisticated intellectual maturity.

THE GOD HYPOTHESIS

With older groups 'The hypothesis box' session affords a great opportunity to explore another of the big questions in philosophy: the question of God's existence. Do 'The God hypothesis' after running the hypothesis session above so that the two contrast.

> **Do:** Write up the following hypothesis:

Hypothesis: *God exists.*

> **Task question:** **How, if at all, can we find out if the hypothesis is true?**

Nested questions

- Is 'the God hypothesis' analogous to 'the object/pineapple hypothesis'? (Are they the same kind of thing?)
- What counts as evidence with the ball example and what counts as evidence with the God example?
- Is evidence necessary for faith?
- Even if you think there is no evidence for God are there any good reasons for believing in God?
- What is it to know God?
- What is it to know that God exists?

Remain sensitive to cultural differences and opinions.

Links

Once Upon an If: Flat Earth; The Island
The Philosophy Shop: Epistemology: Knowledge (section)

THE PEDLAR OF SWAFFHAM

Thinking about thinking about stories

This session is one of the most important in this book as it shows how to apply what is explained in Appendix: The Lost Keys. The PaRDeS method is new to this book and is a method for having children approach the interpretation of stories in a critical mode.

Equipment and preparation needed
- Learn the story to tell (optional)
- Read Appendix: The Lost Keys

Key controversies

What happens in the story? What does the story mean? What do we learn from the story? What does the story represent? What is a legitimate interpretation?

Subject links

Literacy

Key facilitation tool

Critical engagement

Key concepts and vocabulary

Allegory   Moral (noun)
Interpretation   Plot
Meaning   Summary
Metaphor

KEY FACILITATION TOOL

Critical engagement

Engaging young children with validity (an argument's structure) is not at all straightforward. However, getting them into the habit of critically engaging with material and ideas they encounter in school (and then, hopefully, out of it too) is relatively easy to do: just ask them this question: 'Do you agree with X?', or similar questions such as 'What do you think about that?' or 'Do you think it's right?' Or, if you present the class with a quote from Aristotle, for example, say: 'Just because a philosopher said this does not necessarily mean that it's right. What do you think about it? Do you agree with it or not? Why?'

ENGENDERING CRITICAL LITERACY – USING PaRDeS WITH 'THE PEDLAR OF SWAFFHAM'

Note: It is important, before reading or using this session, that you read through Appendix 2 first, as this session provides an example of how to run what is explained more fully there.

The first level of understanding (see Appendix 2) is the *literal level*, or, what *happens* in the story. A risk of asking children to say what happens in a story is that, as any teacher will know, some children can take even longer than the storyteller to recount the events in an '… and then … and then …' way. So, to help circumvent this problem here's what I suggest: for the literal level part of interpreting the story, set the class the following task:

Task question: ▶ **1. Can you say what happens in the story in as few words as possible?**

Do:

1. Pair the children up into As and Bs and give both the As, then the Bs, each one minute to attempt the task.
2. Ask the children to nominate someone (but not themselves); someone they thought did a good job of completing the task.
3. Ask the child nominated to say their summary to the class.
4. Then ask for someone to nominate someone who they thought managed it in even fewer words.
5. Keep going in this way until you get to as succinct a reduction as the class is able to reach.

What's interesting about this method for approaching the literal level is that it not only encourages concision and brevity by urging children to select only the salient features of the plot, it also encourages them to move to the next level of interpretation/understanding: the *moral level*. To show what I mean I will share something that happened in a class of nine- and ten-year-olds I ran this session with. During step 2 (see above) a girl was nominated, who said: 'There was a man who had a dream that he must go to London Bridge. He went there and then met a man who had had a dream that there is a pot of gold hidden …' and so on. She gave a pretty concise summary of the events of the story. Eventually, a boy who had been nominated said, 'Follow your dreams!' Just three words. A disagreement ensued about whether the boy had actually said 'what happens' or whether he had said 'what it's about'. This led to a great discussion about the difference between the two. The children were touching on something the boy had done, though unknowingly; his version had left the literal level and had moved to the *moral level*; in other words, what lesson or moral the reader/audience takes from the story. A stipulation of brevity seems, naturally, to bring about this kind of transition. On this occasion, I used the opportunity to introduce an explicit question, bringing the class to the moral level.

Task question: ▶ **2. What, if anything, do you think we learn from this story?**

A similar, natural move to the *metaphorical level* may happen when you embark on a discussion of the moral level (see Appendix 2 for more on the distinction between the two). Once you have asked TQ2 explicitly, gather and note all the answers on the board. This is what was said in answer to TQ2 by my class of nine- and ten-year-olds:

- Sometimes you should follow your dreams but sometimes you shouldn't.
- Sometimes it is good to follow your dreams but sometimes it is bad to follow your dreams.
- You should trust your instincts.
- Follow your destiny.

One girl, called Maria, noticed that these interpretations led to a problem: 'How do you know *when* it is good to follow your dreams or trust your instincts and how do you know when it's not?' she asked.

Eventually, the discussion led to the following ideas:

- Because your dreams are basically you (because they're in your head), then if you don't trust your dreams you are not trusting yourself.
- It's a battle that you have with yourself.

Understanding the story to represent an inner conflict one has with oneself is an interpretation of the story that has left even the *moral level* and moved to a much deeper *metaphorical/symbolic level*.

THE STORY

This story is one of a few folk-tale versions of a story-type known as 'the man who became rich through a dream'. You will also find a version, among many others, in *The Arabian Nights* tales (there, called 'The ruined man who became rich through a dream').

Say: *There was once a pedlar named John Chapman who lived in a small village called Swaffham – a real town in Norfolk that's still there to this day. John was very poor and, always accompanied by his dog, he spent his time selling small items: ointments, charms or herbal cures and the like whenever he could get them. Sometimes he would make enough money to get a meal and a drink, but other times he did not. He did own a small cottage, but it was dilapidated and without a roof over most of it. However, in the garden of the cottage there grew an apple tree that bore the most delicious apples. If ever he had to go without a meal he could at least eat the apples from his tree.*

One night in a dream, a voice called to him, 'Go to London Bridge! Go to London Bridge!' In the morning he said to himself, 'What a strange dream!' But then he forgot about it. Until, that is, the next night, when he had the very same dream. 'Go to London Bridge!' called the voice again. He was visited by the same dream every night. So haunted by the dream was he that John thought to himself, 'Should I go to London Bridge?'

Task question: **Should he follow the advice of his dream and go to London Bridge?**

Nested questions

• Should you follow the advice of your dreams?

• What is advice?

• What is a dream?

• What do dreams tell us, if anything?

• Where do dreams come from?

Say: *He decided that he would go, if nothing else, to rid himself of the dream. He packed up as many apples as he could carry and set off with his dog. The road to London was long and arduous; the roads in those days being nothing more than dirt tracks. It took him four days to get to London Bridge and when he did arrive he had absolutely no idea what he should do. His dream had instructed him to go there but had said nothing about what to do when he got there. So he decided to wait on the busy bridge all day to see if something would happen. The day eventually came to an end. But had something happened? No. He waited on the bridge a second day. Did anything happen? No.*

He had come such a long way that he decided to wait a third day, and what would have to be his last, as he had run out of apples. As the day was drawing to its close, and just as he had decided to return home to Swaffham, a shopkeeper (for London Bridge, in those days, had shops on it) opened his door and said, 'Excuse me! I have noticed that you have been hanging around for a few days now and today you've sat outside my shop all day. What's going on?'

John said, 'I kept having a dream that told me to go to London Bridge. It was driving me crazy, so I decided to go to London Bridge. And here I am at London Bridge.'

'Are you telling me that you came all the way to London Bridge on the advice of a dream?!' asked the shopkeeper.

John looked down at his feet. 'Yes,' he said.

'You fool!' exclaimed the shopkeeper, 'You should never listen to your dreams. Just last night I had a dream too: I dreamed of a voice that told me to go to a place called – what was it called? Ah! That's right: Swaffham. Never even heard of it! My dream showed me an old dilapidated cottage with no roof. In the back garden was an apple tree and my dream showed me that hidden under the apple tree is buried a pot full of gold. Imagine if I just upped sticks and went in search of a dreamed of pot of gold! Ridiculous! No, if you want my advice, you …'

But when the shopkeeper turned around, John Chapman was gone.

Comprehension question: Where did John Chapman go, and why did he go there?

This is where I choose to end the story, but traditionally there is a resolution. Even if you prefer – or decide for other reasons – to use this 'moral' ending I would still recommend that you stop the story here, and ask the class the comprehension question above. The reason for this is that their answering this question, mentally or verbally, helps them to tie together all the threads of the plot as their minds follow the 'arrow' the story, at this point, has provided. By doing this, they become an active audience, whereas if you simply read the resolution they are passive. I ask the children to turn to each other (using the A/B method described above) and to say where they think John went, and why. Do this whether or not you read the 'moral' ending.

Say: *John hurried home, took out a spade and dug down deep below the tree. Under its roots was a pot that he cracked open with his spade. It spilled open with countless gold coins. John had found his fortune. He rebuilt his home and re-roofed it, purchased all the things he needed to live comfortably, then donated what remained to charity. Each day he would eat an apple from his tree, savouring its flavour. To this day there is a sign in the village of Swaffham that bears a picture of John Chapman and his dog.*

Do: Return to the main task question asked earlier:

Task question: **Should (he) you follow the advice of (his) your dreams?**

See the **Nested question** list above.

Links

More stories to do PaRDeS with (see online resources)

Once Upon an If: The Concept Box

The If Machine: The Meaning of Ant Life; Goldfinger

The If Odyssey: Winged Words; The Words of Tiresias

The Philosophy Shop: Thoth and Thamus; The Questioning Question; Green Ideas; Said and Unsaid; It Started in the Library; C'est de l'or; Jack's Parrot/Windspell; Philosophical Poetry; What We Talk About When We Talk About Words

THE NEVER-ENDING LETTER

Thinking about meaning and interpretation

This is one of the sessions in this book that, among other things, invites the children to respond interpretatively to a stimulus, and it does so by providing the class with a mysterious experience to respond to and make sense of. See my comments about Hermes in the Foreword.

Equipment and preparation needed
- An envelope
- Print off the 'Never-Ending Letter' and place it in the envelope
- Write your class's name on the envelope

Subject links
Literacy

Key controversies
Do stories and poems have single meanings? How many ways can a story or poem be interpreted? Can a story go on forever?

Key facilitation tool
Experience as stimulus (see page 89)

Key concepts and vocabulary
Ellipsis   Mystery
Eternity   Poetry
Infinity   Prose
Meaning

Do: Print off either the 'he' or the 'she' version of the letter. Begin by taking out the envelope and showing the class the letter, the address and the class name on the front. Open the letter and read it to them.

Say:

The Never-Ending Letter

There was once a teacher whose class received a letter from an unknown sender. He opened the letter, then read the letter. His eyes opened in astonishment as he made his way down the page. When he reached the end he looked up again, utterly puzzled and feeling very uneasy.
   'What does it mean?' said the teacher to the class.
   'What does what mean?' one of the children in the class replied.
   The teacher handed the piece of paper to his class for them to look at. One of the pupils took it and began to read out loud. The pupil said:

Do: At this point pass the story to a pupil in the class who should then read the story, acting out being the teacher, then handing it to another pupil who repeats this procedure. Stop when it's clear that this will go on.

> ### *The Never-Ending Letter*
>
> *There was once a teacher whose class received a letter from an unknown sender. He opened the letter then read the letter. His eyes opened in astonishment as he made his way down the page. When he reached the end he looked up again, utterly puzzled and feeling uneasy.*
> *'What does it mean?' said the teacher to the class.*
> *'What does what mean?' one of the children in the class replied.*
> *The teacher handed the piece of paper to his class for them to look at. One of the pupils took the piece of paper and began to read out loud. The pupil said:*
>
> ### *The Never-Ending Letter*
>
> *There was once a teacher whose class received a letter from an unknown sender …*

Comprehension question: Can you say what happens in this story?

Nested questions

• Why is it called 'The Never-Ending Letter'?

Hermeneutic question: What do you think this story means?

Nested questions

• Is 'what the story means' the same as 'what happens in the story'?
• Does this story have just one meaning?
• Does this story have many meanings?
• Does this story have any meanings at all?
• How do you know what the meaning of a story or poem is?
• How can you decide what the right meaning of a story or poem is?
• Does a story or poem have a correct meaning?
• Can you be wrong about what you think a story or poem means?
• What is meaning?
• What does 'meaning' mean?
• What is interpretation? Is it the same as meaning?
• Am I in this story?
• Are you in this story?
• Can we be both in and out of the story at the same time?

Task question: **What is the Never-Ending Letter?**

Nested questions

• Is it a story? A poem? A letter? Or something else?

More on interpretation

Try the PaRDeS procedure (see Appendix 2), or elements of it, with this story.

Meaning

What do the following sentences mean?

- 'The cat sat on the mat.'
- 'A green thought in a green shade.' – Andrew Marvell
- 'The slithy toves did gyre and gimble in the wabe.' – Lewis Carroll
- 'Green ideas sleep furiously.' – Noam Chomsky
- 'What does this sentence mean?'
- 'This sentence does not mean what it says it means.'

Foreverness

Which of the following go on forever?

- 1, 2, 3, 4, 5, 6, 7, 8, 9, 10, 11, 12 … and so on
- a, b, c, d, e, f, g, h, i, j, k, l, m, n … and so on
- 0, -1, -2, -3, -4, -5, -6, -7, -8, -9, -10, -11 … and so on
- … -5, -4, -3, -2, -1, 0, 1, 2, 3, 4, 5, 6, 7 … and so on (in both directions)
- Outer space
- Inner space
- Time
- The past
- The future
- The present
- The story 'The Never-Ending Letter', above
- Your mind
- (Pi) 3.14159265359 …
- 33.333333 recurring …

Links

Once Upon an If: Once Upon an If (parts 1 and 2); The Matches – Extension activity 5: Flash-fiction; It

The If Machine: The Meaning of Ant Life; The Little Old Shop of Curiosities; To the Edge of Forever; Get Stuffed

The If Odyssey: The Concealer (TQ: Would you take up Kalypso's offer to live forever?)

The Library of Babel by Jorge Luis Borges

The Numberverse: Inbetweeny bits; A bit more than 3

The Philosophy Shop: Metaphysics: Fiction, Language and Meaning or What Can Be Said About What There Is

Thoughtings: A Town Called That; Without an 'M' in the alphabet …; How Long is a String of Letters?; Infinity Add One; A Disappearing Riddle

THE INCREDIBLE SHRINKING MACHINE

26

Thinking about the microcosm

*This session is a development of a short passage from **The If Machine** (page 187). It is reasonably involved but a lot of fun, and very engaging when done in the way described. It is a great way to have the children think about the microcosm and will work to supplement any curriculum area that, in some way, deals with the world of the tiny and unseen, such as dissolving, evaporation, cells and so on.*

Equipment and preparation needed

- A chair
- Something to act as a 'computer' (it can be, but doesn't have to be, a computer)
- Prepare the talk-circle
- A board that everyone can see

Subject links

Maths
Science (microscopes, dissolving, evaporation)

Key controversies

Can a thing be composed of smaller things *ad infinitum*? Is there a smallest thing?

Key concepts and vocabulary

Composition	Existence
Disappear	Infinity
Disintegrate	Nothing
Divisibility	Seeing
Exist	Substance

Possible misconception

That disappearing means not existing

Key facilitation tool

Random number generator

KEY FACILITATION TOOL

Random number generator

I use this device a good deal. When, as in 'The incredible shrinking machine', you are likely to get lots of children who want to volunteer, but only a limited number that can take part, then use random selection methods. I have an app on my phone that selects numbers randomly between a given range.

1. Have all the children, starting from one end of the talk-circle, say a number consecutively from 1 to n, ending at the other end of the circle. Tell the children to remember their number.

2. Set the number range on your 'random number generator' app. For example, 1–28.

3. Press the button that activates the 'generate number' function.

4. Call out the number. The child whose number it is, is selected.

INTRODUCE THE INCREDIBLE SHRINKING MACHINE

Do: Begin by placing a chair in the middle of the room.

Say: I want you to imagine that the chair is a futuristic machine that shrinks things and people to any size: an 'incredible shrinking machine'. There are wires coming out of it, connecting it to a super-computer.

Do: Use your own computer to stand in for this. Indicate towards it.

Say: It is surrounded by a glass booth and there's a sliding door so you can get in and out.

Do: Take any object in the room, such as a book, and place it in the chair.

Say: First of all, we must decide on a size for the object to be shrunk to. Let's say the size of an egg. Then I programme in the size and press 'Go'. It starts to shrink.

Do: Do all the appropriate actions, either at the 'computer' or the 'machine', as you describe or explain them, then make a special noise to indicate that something is shrinking.

Say: I can see what size the object or person is on my computer. When it reaches the requested size I press 'Stop'. Then I press 'Original size' for it to go back to the size it started at.

SHRINK TWO CHILDREN

Say: Would anyone like to have a go?

Do: Utilise the random number generator (see box) to randomly select someone to have a go in the 'incredible shrinking machine'.

Say: First of all, you will need to put on a special suit and helmet [hand an imaginary suit to them]. This will protect you as you shrink so that your air supply shrinks with you, making the journey perfectly safe. It also has a speaking unit so that we can all hear you perfectly well here in the laboratory, whatever size you are. Next, you need to decide how small you want to be shrunk.

Do: Help the children with this sentence-starter: 'I would like to be shrunk to the size of a …' Remind them that they are not *turned into* whatever it is, they will just be the same size. Have them undergo the process you described above. When they have been shrunk, ask them to step out and describe the world as they see it. Ask questions to encourage them, if necessary, such as:

- 'What's the carpet like, from the point of view of something the size of an X [insert object size they requested]?'
- 'How do you feel when you look up?'
- 'What's your journey to school like?' etc.

You may want to repeat this activity with one more volunteer (depending on the available time).

THE INCREDIBLE SHRINKING MACHINE ADVENTURE

Say: We don't have time for everyone to sit on this chair, so I want you all to imagine that the chair you are sitting on is an 'incredible shrinking machine'. First of all, put on your suits! Now put on your helmets! Now decide what size you would like to be.

Do: Have some of them say how small they would like to be. Ask, after each contribution, if there is anyone who would be even smaller. This encourages them to stretch their imaginations towards the smallest things they are able to think of. Note the suggestions on the board. Move to the controls and …

Say: I am going to set the controls to your requested size. Now, I'm going to press 'Go'.

Do: Make the special noise to indicate that they are shrinking. Be ready for them to roll up and go on the floor!

Say: You're reaching the requested size, so I'm going to press 'Stop' NOW! Oh no! It's not working, the machine seems to be broken. You are continuing to shrink and shrink and shrink!

Do: Tell them all to sit back on their chairs, ready for a philosophy discussion. Ask the following start-question.

Start question: What is going to happen?

At some point you will probably want to move to a more philosophical task question. Be on the look-out for good *emergent questions* (see page xi) coming from the children, or introduce the most appropriate and relevant question from the list of questions below, most of which have come from children at some point.

Task question: Can something be so small that it can't exist? (Alice, aged 8)

Nested questions
- How small will you get?
- Will you continue to get smaller for ever?
- Is there a size where you can't get any smaller?
- Will you disappear?
- If so, what does 'disappear' mean?
- Does 'disappear' mean 'no longer exist' or does it mean 'can no longer be seen'?
- What's the difference between these two?
- Would you shrink to nothing? What does 'shrink to nothing' mean?

Questioning hint: A useful question to *if* with and *anchor* to is: 'If you did keep shrinking, would you shrink forever?' This question helps the group to follow the philosophical line of enquiry without getting stuck on red herrings such as 'but you would die'.

EXTENSION ACTIVITY

Once the enquiry described above has been allowed to develop, you may want to set the class any or some of the following tasks:

The ... est thing

- Think of the smallest thing you can.
- Think of the biggest thing you can.

Then set the children the task of thinking of something even smaller/bigger. Examples I have heard include, 'heaven', 'God', 'nothing', 'something', 'universe', 'atom', etc. Return to the list of suggestions you made earlier and ask them to decide which of the things listed is the smallest/biggest, e.g. 'atom', 'cell', 'dust', etc. This could lead to a good research question (see page 119).

Ten things

Ask the class to list ten things they know are in the room but that they cannot see (even if they were to look). Examples, 'thoughts', 'air', 'heat', 'germs', etc.

Seeing the unseen

Show microscopic images from the Internet such as the tongue's surface, head lice, an eggshell, or anything that looks very different when magnified. Ask the following task question:

Task question: **At what size do we see things as they really are?**

(See 'Reality glasses' on page 119 to extend this further.)

Explain that there are some things that are so small we can't even see them with a microscope.
Research question: Can you find any examples of things that are so small we can't see them even with a microscope?

Task question: **How do we know something is there if we cannot see it (even through a microscope)?**

Links

'The Indefatigable Frog' by Philip K. Dick (ask the TQ at the right time in the story.
Task question: Will the frog ever get to the end of the tube?)
Alice's Adventures in Wonderland by Lewis Carroll: Chapter 1 'Down the Rabbit Hole', the 'Drink Me' episode. (**Task question:** Will Alice go out like a candle?)
Once Upon an If: The Six Wise Men; Water People
The If Machine: The Chair; Thinking About Nothing; To the Edge of Forever; Get Stuffed
The Philosophy Shop: Immy's Box; A Heap of Exercises?; A Pageful of Nothing; Phil and Soph and the Ice Cream; The Philosophical Adventures of Pencil Person
Thoughtings: Atoms; Littlest; Mostly Made of Space

THE INSTANT SUCCESS SWITCH

Thinking about talents, skills and virtues

Inspired by Plato's Meno dialogue (see below) this session is designed to think through, but also to link together, the concepts of talent, skill and virtue. Can being a good person be taught? If so, how? Participants may also, along the way, learn something about what matters to them – what their values are.

Equipment and preparation needed

- An object that can act as a switch that can be placed in the centre of the room, or draw/make a 'switch' on a piece of A4 paper

Subject links

Literacy
PSHE

Key controversies

If effort is not necessary is effort still worth anything?

Key facilitation tool

Conceptual comparisons (see page 110)

Key concepts and vocabulary

Commitment	Skill
Effort	Style
Good person	Talent
Learning	Virtue

Do: Place 'the switch' in the centre of the room.

Say: Think of someone who has a skill or talent that you would like to have that you don't think you have now. It can be anyone: someone famous or someone you know personally.

Do: Gather candidates (e.g. a parent, a celebrity, a sportsperson, a friend and so on) and record some of the answers (or all if you prefer).

Say: Imagine that the switch you see on the floor is an 'instant success switch'. If you press it then you will instantly have the skills and/or talents of the person you selected, exactly as they have them, without having to practise, train or have a natural talent. For example, if you wanted to be able to sing like Beyoncé then, by pressing the switch, you will be able to sing just like Beyoncé, or if you wanted to be able to play football like Ronaldo then, by pressing the switch, you will be able to play football just like Ronaldo.

Nested questions

- What reasons could there be for pressing the switch?
- Are there any reasons not to press the switch?
- Are practice and training good things to do?
- What is a skill? Make a list of some skills.
- What is a natural talent? Make a list of some natural talents.
- Can you gain/improve skills through practice and training?
- Can you gain/improve natural talents through practice and training?
- If you don't *need* to practise or train, is there any reason why you might *choose* to practise or train?

Here's what the dictionary says about 'skill' and 'talent':

Skill: *special ability in a particular field, especially acquired by learning and practice*

Talent: *the natural abilities of a person, especially a person's general intelligence or mental power* Longman's Dictionary of The English Language

Do: Introduce these definitions when appropriate, but not too early in the discussion, giving the children time to explore their own conceptions before introducing the standard ones. Ask the start-question again:

Start question: **Would you press the switch?**

(See Nested question list above.)

Instant success switch variations

To make the thought-experiment more focused, here are some suggested variations for the 'instant success switch' (feel free to add more):

- Instant musician – choose any musician or singer and press the button to instantly have all their skill, technique and style. Would you press it?
- Instant explorer
- Instant bestselling writer
- Instant multi-linguist
- Instant Olympic gold medallist

Do some conceptual analysis (see 'Conceptual analysis' on page 110) around the concepts *skill*, *talent*, *technique*, *style*.

Meno's question

Say: In a dialogue called the Meno, written by the ancient Greek philosopher Plato, the eponymous character, Meno, asks the character Socrates a question at the outset about whether virtue can be taught.

Meno: Can you tell me, Socrates, can virtue be taught?
Or is it not teachable but the result of practice, or is it neither
of these, but men possess it by nature or in some other way?

(Translated by G.M.A. Grube)

Task question: **1. Can we be taught to be good people?**

Task question: **2. Does being a good person come from training and practice or birth and nature? Or somewhere else?**

Say: 'Virtue' is those characteristics that make a person a good person. For example, the main virtues of the ancient Greeks were:

- Knowledge
- Wisdom
- Temperance (self-control)
- Piety (holiness)
- Courage

Do: Try the 'instant success switch' thought-experiment (above) with virtue instead: the 'instant good switch'.

The Good School

Say: Imagine a school that has been set up to teach people how to be good people.

Task question: What lessons should be taught in order for the students to learn to be good people?

The Smart Pill

There's been talk for some time now about a 'smart pill'. It has been said that there will soon be a pill that can be taken to make us smarter.

Task question: Would you and should you take smart pills?

Links

Mr. Good by Roger Hargreaves

Once Upon an If: The Promise Slippers; The Luckiest Man in the World

The If Machine: The Ring of Gyges; The Frog and the Scorpion; Billy Bash; Friends

The If Odyssey: The Hero; The Storyteller

The Philosophy Shop: Perfect People; Arete and Deon; The Pill of Life

TPF website: 'The Perfect School' by Oliver Leech

Conceptual comparisons

Take two words that are similar, or related in some way, and ask whether they are the same or different. For instance:

- Mind, brain
- Ice, water
- Skill, talent (as in the instant success switch)
- Person, human
- Think, know

You could do this in reverse. How many different kinds of X can you find for the following?

- Free (e.g. physical freedom or freedom of thought or expression …)
- Love
- Time
- Happiness
- Truth

(See 'Carve it up!' on page 30, 'Break the circle' on page 54, and 'Ropes and hoops' on page 37 for more conceptual analysis tools.) Even if you go to the dictionary afterwards, conceptual analysis can help diagnose the children's understanding of the relevant concepts.

Conceptual analysis

Analysing concepts is thinking about the meanings that lie behind a word or an idea. A word is used to represent or help us express a concept or concepts. A good place to start conceptual analysis is to ask, 'What is X?'. Some concepts fit together nicely: the concept of husband and the concept of wife are made for each other. Others, however, do not. What is 6 divided by 0? Or, for that matter, what is any number divided by 0? The concept of natural numbers and the concept(s) of division by zero just don't work together. The brain aches to think about it. In philosophy, trouble arises when concepts don't easily fit together. The concepts of causation and free will, mind and brain, religion and science, justice and power are just a few corresponding sides to conceptual coins that, once you start to think about, difficulties arise. Philosophers are good at identifying problems in concepts (the philosopher Simon Blackburn describes philosophers as 'conceptual engineers') where many of us would not see a problem. Stopping and asking ourselves, 'What is X?' is the first step to seeing a problem? Sharing ideas with others and listening to theirs, is the next.

Iffing the fact/Either-or-the-if

Sometimes, empirical facts get in the way of a good discussion. 'Can we time travel?', 'They can't do brain transplants', 'Do all our cells get replaced every seven years?', 'It wouldn't be possible to get everyone to vote', etc. These are just some of the factual issues that come up during philosophy sessions. Whatever you do, don't get drawn in! Instead, employ the conceptual techniques of the 'armchair philosopher' (see page 113): simply 'if' these facts like so: 'If everyone could vote and everyone voted that the *Mona Lisa* was the most beautiful painting, then would it be?' (See 'Art detectives' on page 145); or 'If we were able to time travel then would you choose to do something other than you did the first time?' In some cases you may need to extend this technique a little; you may need to 'either-or-the-if': 'Let's think about it both ways: if all our cells *are* replaced every seven years then would you be the same person after ten years?' Then 'go the other way': 'And if our cells are *not* all replaced, but only, say, 70% of them are, then would you be the same person after ten years?'

Links

See 'If the fact and if the idea' on page 35 of *The If Machine* and 'Either/or the if' on pages 42 and 174 of *The If Machine* for more on these strategies.

THE TIME MACHINE

Thinking about time and time travel

Again, here the 'disappointing, magic trick' device (see page 62) is used to create a response to instigate a discussion. But in this case, arguably, you will not be telling fibs, because the 'time traveller' really will be travelling into the future, just in a 'boring way'. Or is it?

Equipment and preparation needed

- A chair
- A clock, watch or stopwatch
- Have the film *The Time Machine* (1960, rated PG) ready (optional)
- Have the Time-phone ready to project or handout (see online)

Subject links

Literacy
(science fiction)
Science

Key controversies

Is time itself different from time-measuring devices? Are we time travellers?

Key concepts and vocabulary

Future	Present
Now	Time
Past	Time travel

Possible misconception

That *time* is the same as 'the measurement of time', such as a clock

Key facilitation tool

Iffing the fact/Either-or-the-if on page 111

Do: Place a chair in the middle of the room.

Say: Is there anyone who would like to be a time-traveller?

Do: Choose a volunteer (see 'Random number generator' on page 101).

Say: You are going to travel through time into the future on this [gesture towards the chair] TIME MACHINE! Choose a time period to travel to. Any time at all, as long as it is in the future; this time machine is not able to travel into the past, I'm afraid. The other thing is that it is not a very powerful time machine, so you can only travel to anywhere between one and ten seconds into the future. So, choose a time!

Do: Once the children have chosen their future time to travel to (somewhere between one and ten seconds into the future), invite them to sit in 'the time machine'. Hold up your watch or stopwatch and have the rest of the class count the number of seconds between one and ten that the time traveller chose. Then, to 'the time traveller'…

Say: Well done! You have now travelled X [insert the number of seconds they chose] seconds into the future! How does it feel to be in the future?

Task question: **1. Did [insert student's name] travel into the future?**

Nested questions

- If yes, why or how?
- If no, why not?
- Did they travel through time?
- Are we always travelling through time?
- Are we always moving into the future?

Task question: **2. If the chair is not a time machine, then what *would* be a time machine?**

Nested questions

- If yes, why or how?
- If no, why not?
- Did they travel through time?
- Are we always travelling through time?
- Are we always moving into the future?

A LITTLE PHILOSOPHY

Armchair philosophy

There are some philosophers who think that the question as to whether time travel is possible or not is a logical issue not a scientific one. If time travel leads to a logical contradiction (P and not P) then, argue those philosophers, it is not and never will be possible. Yes, flight was considered impossible by some before it was achieved, but that was never a logical problem, just a question of technology. For these 'logical' philosophers, if time travel leads to a contradiction, then time travel is as possible as that the sum 2 + 2 = 5 could be true.

Changing the future 1

Say: What do you think you will be doing in 20 seconds' time? Sitting down, perhaps? Let's see! When the second hand gets to the [insert number 20 seconds from now] I want everyone to stand up.

Start question: Does the fact that we all stood up mean that we changed the future?

Changing the future 2

Say: This time, when the second hand gets to the [insert number 20 seconds from now] I want everyone to either stand up or stay sat down; you decide!

Start question: Does the fact that you each decided for yourself what to do mean that you changed the future?

Task question: Can you change your own future?

Nested question

• Can you create your own future?

The time-phone

Do: Show (project or hand out) the following piece of writing to the class:

Say: I am writing these words at 7.14pm on 2 February, 2015. You will be reading these words in my future but your present. We are connecting through time. The act of writing is like a time-phone. However, it only goes in one direction: from me to you; you can't speak back to me, but you can hear me. So, I have a question for you: is writing a time-travelling device, a doorway through time, a time-phone? It is now 7.20pm. Or is it?

Links

100 World Myths and Legends by Geraldine McCaughrean: The Armchair Traveller

101 Philosophy Problems by Martin Cohen: Section on Time and time travel

Alice's Adventures in Wonderland by Lewis Carroll: Chapter 5: A Mad Tea-Party

Doctor Who and Philosophy: Timey-Wimey Stuff by Peter Worley

Once Upon an If: Flat Earth

The If Machine: The Little Old Shop of Curiosities

The If Odyssey: Under the World; The Horror of the Rocks

The Philosophy Files by Stephen Law: Chapter 5: Is Time Travel Possible?; *The Philosophy Shop*: Metaphysics: Time

Thoughtings: From Me to You; Petering; A Time Machine; Light From Stars; Possible World?

WHEN WORLDS COLLIDE

Thinking about dilemmas

Based on the 1950s science fiction film of the same name, this is a version of the classic 'balloon debate'. Remember, that though Task question 1 is very engaging, in order to get to the philosophy in this session it is important to ask Task question 2. These two questions provide a good example of what might be called a 'surface-level question' (TQ1) and a 'deeper-level question' (TQ2).

Equipment and preparation needed
- Scrap paper for the group activity below
- Have the film *When Worlds Collide* (1951, rated U) ready (optional)

Subject links
PSHE

Key controversies
Are people of equal value? When might someone think that they're not?

Key facilitation tool
Iffing, anchoring and opening up (see pages 53)

Key concepts and vocabulary
Consequences   Dilemma
Decisions   Ethics

KEY FACILITATION TOOL

Iffing, anchoring and opening up
You will need to anchor the class to the parameters of the dilemma: 'And if you *had* to choose between the two, which would you choose? And why?' (see page 53).

Do: Explain that you are going to put the children *into* a science fiction story (see Once Upon an If pages 79-82). Remind them that it is fiction.

Say: Imagine that the world is going to end. A huge asteroid is going to collide with Earth, destroying it and all life depending on it. Scientists, in the time available to them, have been able to build a space rocket that will take people to another planet, Earth 2, a planet that has recently been discovered, that – it turns out – is able to support human life. Those on board will have to be put into cryogenic suspension to reach the planet, as it is many hundreds of light years away. The problem is that the short amount of time between identifying just how destructive the asteroid will be and the point of impact, is not long – just a matter of weeks. So, only ONE spacecraft has been built in that time and it can only carry 12 people.

Task question: 1. Who should go? Why?

Nested questions

- Should it be 'first come, first served'?
- Should it be those who funded it who decide?
- Should the wise and knowledgeable go?
- Should the young or the old go?
- Should *you* be allowed to go?

GROUP ACTIVITY

Say: In groups of four or five, make a list of 12 people that should take their places on the spacecraft, and provide reasons for why they should be allowed to go.

Do: Have the groups offer their lists and justify *why* they have chosen who they have. Conduct the main enquiry around these discussions and any disagreements.

Task question: 2. How should *who goes* be decided?

Nested questions

- On what basis should the decision be made?
- Should it be something like usefulness? How nice they are? How young they are? Or some other principle?
- Should it be decided randomly?

EXTENSION ACTIVITY

New situations

Feel free to come up with your own new situations that create new dilemmas or controversies. Here are a few ideas to get you started:

THE TAKEN PLACE

Say: It turns out that, of the 12 places there are only 11 to decide, because the person who funded the building of the spacecraft has secured his or her own survival by taking the first place.

Task question: Is it right that the person who funded the rocket should automatically get a place?

SABOTAGE!

Say: Two people attempt to blow up the spaceship. They are caught just in time and their plan is foiled. When questioned, they each give different reasons for their actions: the first says, 'It's not fair that such a small group should go; it's fairer that no one goes.'

Task question: Do you agree with the saboteur's reason?

Say: The second saboteur gives the following reason: 'We should not contaminate another planet as we have done this one.'

Task question: Do you agree with the second saboteur's reason?

Do: Show the film *When Worlds Collide*, or extracts from it, to get the children talking or to accompany some of the scenarios above.

Links

101 Ethical Dilemmas by Martin Cohen

Games for Thinking by Robert Fisher: Balloon Debate; Red or Black?

Once Upon an If: The Sindbad Stories

The If Machine: The Lie; The Prince and the Pig; The Ring of Gyges; Republic Island; The Little Old Shop of Curiosities; The Shadow of the Pyramid

The If Odyssey: Happiness and Forgetting; Captain or Crew?; Choices; The Horror of the Rocks; Clouded

The Philosophy Shop: The Wicked Which; A Bad Picture; The Pill of Life; Charlie's Choice; The Salesman; Buridan's Asteroid

Thoughtings: The Wicked Which; Naughty-Land

REALITY GLASSES

Thinking about perception

A more challenging session on two of the old favourites of philosophy: perception and reality, often parodied with the famous musing, 'How do I know this glass is really here?' You may be surprised just how sophisticated the children can be with this session.

Equipment and preparation needed
- A pair of glasses (I use a pair of old sunglasses with the lenses taken out)

Subject links
Art
Science

Key controversies
Is it possible to perceive reality *as it is*?

Key facilitation tool
Research questions

Key concepts and vocabulary
Composition
Objective
Perception
Perspective
Point of view

Reality
Seeing
Subjective
Truth

KEY FACILITATION TOOL

Research questions
Because examples and counter-examples are often real-world based, they will often lead to what I call 'research questions'. Sometimes a discussion calls for a fact to be known. Ask the children to find out, for instance, whether a molecule or an atom is smaller, or to find out exactly how the eye works (see below). This is one clear and easy way that philosophy can be linked to the curriculum, and it shows how a 'love of wisdom' can lead to a 'love of knowledge'. Only after I had left school did I re-discover an interest in history, maths and science – through reading philosophy. (See also 'Iffing the fact/either-or-the-if' on page 111.)

Do: Place the glasses in the centre of the talk-circle.

Say: Let's imagine that these are special glasses; they have been made by super-clever scientists. These scientists wanted to know what the world is really like. So they have made these 'reality glasses'. They enable the wearer to see the world as it really is.

Nested questions

- What is seeing?
- What is reality?
- Can you see reality as it really is? This is a 'welcome assumptions' (see page 130).
- What would it be to see things as they really are?

Do: Allow the discussion to unfold for a while and, only if necessary, move to the following question:

Task question: Do we *already* see things as they really are?

Nested questions

- How would you know when what you see is really 'how it is' and not just 'how you see it'?
- Are our eyes 'reality glasses'?
- How do we see? (This could be a *research question*.)

EXTENSION ACTIVITY

Putting on the glasses

Say: It's time to put on the reality glasses. If you were to put them on and then look at the following things what would you see, if you were seeing them as they really are?

- The famous duck–rabbit illusion (easily available online). **TQ:** Is it really a duck, or a rabbit, or is it really something else?
- Other illusions such as the Necker cube. **TQ:** Is it really a cube?
- A painting such as Monet's *Waterlilies* and/or Matsys' *The Ugly Duchess*. **TQ:** Is it really beautiful/ugly?

Senses

Say: Some animals don't see very well and, in some cases, they don't see at all. However, they very often have at least one other sense that is far better developed than our own. For instance, many bats can hear much better than we can, snakes have a sense of taste that enables them to 'see' with their tongue, wolves have a heightened sense of smell and spiders can often sense movement very acutely indeed.

Task question: Are any of the senses more important than the others for being able to see the world *as it really is*?

Nested questions

- What is a sense?
- What do senses do?
- Could there be more senses than 'the five senses'? (This could be a research question.)
- If you had to lose a sense, which would you opt to lose first? Then second, third, fourth and fifth?
- If you were able to improve just one sense, which would it be?
- If you could choose one sense from five animals, which sense, from which animal, would you choose?

Links

Once Upon an If: The Six Wise Men; Water People; Flat Earth; Honest Sa'id; The Island
The If Machine: The Chair; Get Stuffed
The Philosophy Shop: Epistemology: Perception, especially The Duck and Rabbit; The Goodness Detector; The Beauty Detector
Thoughtings: Are Things Always What They Seem To Us To Be?
Any good illusions book

PERSPECTACLES

Thinking about point-of-view and perspective

Like 'Reality glasses' this makes use of glasses as a prop and it is a more challenging session. I recommend following the guidelines carefully to help bring the children to the problem of swapping points-of-view. If they have difficulty with the first exercise go straight to the Hodja story.

Equipment and preparation needed
• Two pairs of fake glasses, ideally of different designs

Subject links
PSHE

Key controversies
To what extent, if any, can we see things outside of our own perspective?

Key facilitation tool
The imaginary disagreer

Key concepts and vocabulary
Consciousness	Point of view
Empathy	Self
Perspective	

KEY FACILITATION TOOL

The imaginary disagreer: putting on the perspectacles

This is a strategy for activating the children to seek an alternative point of view. Simply ask, 'If there was someone who disagreed with you, what do you think they might say?' and, if necessary, follow this up with 'And what reasons do you think they might give?' (See 'Facilitating idea-diversity' in Appendix 1 for more on this.)

Say: Today, let's imagine that these [gesture towards your props] are spectacles that either magically or scientifically have a very unusual power; they enable the wearers to perceive – or see – the world from each other's point of view, or perspective. Because they enable you to swap perspectives with other people, they are called 'perspectacles'.

Do: Now ask for two volunteers, A and B, to come to the front of the room, and for each of them to stand behind one pair of the perspectacles.

Say: First of all, put on your perspectacles in order to allow them to take in (somehow absorb) your point of view. Now, swap perspectacles with each other. You now have the other person's point of view. [Insert volunteer A's name], you see things how [insert volunteer B's name] sees things and you [insert volunteer B's name], see things how [insert volunteer A's name] sees things. What does the world look like from each other's point of view?

Do: Here are some tasks to help the children find their way around this – quite difficult – idea. It may be a good idea to ask for new volunteers between each of the tasks, especially if one student doesn't understand and someone else thinks they do:

- Tell them to stand in front of each other and ask them who it is they each see.
- Ask one of them to move slowly around the space in the room. Ask the other one what they are seeing or experiencing.
- Ask one of them to spin around. Ask the other one what they are seeing or experiencing.
- Ask one to look up at the ceiling and the other to look down at the ground. Ask them each what they see.

A useful question to 'if' with: Whenever you ask them to report on these tasks, always insert 'if you are seeing the world from each other's point of view …' before adding 'what/who are you seeing?' This reminds them of the special conditions the thought-experiment confers.

Task question: **Is it possible to see things from someone else's point-of-view?**

Nested questions

- If you were to see through someone else's point of view, would that mean that you are them?
- Is swapping points of view just the same as swapping eyes?
- Do you need the perspectacles to be able to gain someone else's point of view?
- Is it possible, or might it one day be possible, to become someone else?
- Do you swap points of view with someone if you: Swap eyes? Swap brains? Swap bodies?

EXTENSION ACTIVITY

Different points of view

Say: What would the world be like from the point of view of … (and what would your point of view be like to …):

- Your best friend?
- Someone of the opposite gender?
- Someone from a different culture?
- An android/robot?
- A dog? A bat?

- A tree?
- A single-celled organism?
- A rock?
- The Sun?
- God?

Task question: **Do all/some/none of the above have a point of view?**

Start by reading the introduction to the Hodja on page 72. Then read the following story:

 A Turban Tale

One night, the Hodja is travelling somewhere and he stays overnight at an inn. While he is sleeping, some of the other travellers, also staying at the inn, think that it would be funny to take off his turban and swap it with another sleeping traveller's turban; a much smaller one. When the Hodja wakes up and sees the man wearing his turban he says, 'If that man over there is me, then who am I?'

Task question: **If someone else were who you are, then who would you be?**

Nested questions

- Can someone else be you? Can you be someone else?
- What does the Hodja think here? Is he confused? If so, how?
- Is there anything wrong with the way the Hodja is thinking?
- Do your clothes at all determine who you are?
- Do your clothes at all determine how other people see you?
- What would you need to swap with someone in order to be someone else? Is it even possible?

Links

Once Upon an If: Bite and sting: tense and person for thinking; Once Upon an If (parts 1 and 2 and story-writing activity); Flat Earth

The If Machine: Where Are You?; The Prince and the Pig; Yous on Another Planet; The Android

The If Odyssey: Nobody's Home; The Horror of the Rocks; Tenses and Persons

The Philosophy Shop: The Copying Machine

Thoughtings: An Other Poem; From Me to You; The Yeah-Coz-Fingee; Who's That?; Thing-a-Me!; That's Me!

TRUING AND LYING

Thinking about truth and lies

Even intelligent adult groups I run this session with often revise their view of what constitutes a lie. Many will begin by thinking that a lie is simply saying something false, only later realising that there are many ways one can say something false without lying, for instance, an honest mistake, telling a story or children's make-believe play. What will you learn or revise about truth and lies during this session? (See 'Possible misconceptions' on page x)

Equipment and preparation needed

- Two items that can function as 'magic' items – I use a necklace and a glass crystal
- An ordinary item such as a pen or pencil
- A box with a ball placed inside and a piece of paper stuck to the outside of the box with a rough picture of a ball drawn on it

Subject links

Literacy
PSHE
RE
Science

Key controversies

Is 'telling the truth' the same as 'saying what is true'? Is there a difference between lying and being mistaken? Is there a difference between lying and saying something false?

Possible misconception

That lying is simply saying what is false and that saying 'what is true' is the same as 'telling the truth'

Key concepts and vocabulary

Belief	Make-believe
Joke	Mistake
Knowledge	Sincerity
Lies	Truth

Key facilitation tool

Closed questioning for focus

KEY FACILITATION TOOL

Closed questioning for focus

I used to find it difficult to focus many of the discussions following a stimulus until I discovered the virtue of asking grammatically closed questions as task questions (see Appendix 1). During this session, make sure you regularly come back to the main TQ below: 'Did A say the truth and did B lie?' You may want to use the *atomic questioning* strategy (see 'Atomic questioning' on page 72): 'So, did A say the truth?' and then, 'Did B lie?' I use the expression 'say the truth', so that it leaves it more open; saying 'tell the truth' can lead them to understand 'truth' only as 'sincerity'. A good follow-up strategy to this is to use a *response detector* (see Appendix 1) like so: 'Is there anyone who thinks that A didn't say the truth/B didn't lie?' Just remember to open closed questions up again! (See Appendix 1.)

DO: Place the two 'magic items' on the floor in the middle of the talk-circle next to each other.

Say: I want you to imagine that these two items are magic; for the rest of the session I will therefore refer to them as magic. The necklace [or whatever it is] is a necklace of truth. Whoever wears it or holds it always says the truth. The stone [or whatever it is] is a stone of lying. Whoever holds it always lies. I will need two volunteers.

Do: Select two volunteers using a random selection method (see 'Random number generator' on page 101) – A and B [insert pupils' names] – and have them put on or hold the items, one for each of the volunteers.

THE OBJECT

Do: Place an uncontroversial and unambiguous object on the floor in front of the volunteers, such as a pen or pencil.

Say: What have I put on the floor in front of you?

Do: Write up on the board what each of the volunteers said, along with their name [e.g. A said, while holding the necklace of truth: 'A pen.' B, while holding the lying stone: 'A chicken.'] Ask them to put the items back on the floor and then to sit down again.

Task question: Did A say the truth and did B lie?

Nested questions
- What is truth?
- What is a lie?
- Is 'telling the truth' the same or different from 'saying what is true'? (sincerity/objectivity distinction)
- Is lying different from saying what is not true? (deception/falsity distinction and error/intentional-deception distinction)
- Is it a lie if you are made to lie (by a magic stone, for instance)?
- Is deceiving for a joke the same as a lie? (wicked intent/non-wicked intent distinction)
- Is children pretending that something is other than it is, when playing for example, the same as lying?

THE BOX AND THE BALL

Do: Show the class the box you've prepared, but do not reveal that there is anything in it. Instead draw their attention to the drawing on the box. Ask them what they think it's a drawing of. It's good if the drawing is a little ambiguous so that some think it's a ball and others think it's like the Moon, or something …

Say: I'm going to need two more volunteers!

Do: Place the box in front of the two volunteers.

Say: Is there a ball in front of you?

Do: Ask the TQ again:

Task question: Did A say the truth and did B lie?

Nested questions
- Is a drawing of a ball a ball?
- If you think the drawing is of something else (e.g. the Moon), is it a ball?
- If the artist meant for it to be a ball, is it a ball?

Do: At some point during the discussion open the box to reveal that there is, in fact, a ball in the box. Then ask the following task question:

Task question: Does that mean that A, in fact, lied and that B, in fact, said the truth? (This question will depend on what they did, in fact, say.)

Nested questions
- Can you lie by accident?
- Can you say the truth by accident?
- If the necklace makes you 'say the truth' what do you think the necklace should have made A say?
- What is 'the truth'?

More situations

Here are some more situations that involve lying or saying the truth to try with your 'magic items'. Feel free to invent your own examples.

The Christmas jumper

Say: As a present, your grandmother gives you a jumper she has knitted for you. You do not like it. She asks you, 'what do you think?'

Start question: If you are wearing the necklace of truth, what would you say?

Task question: What would be the right thing to say if you were not wearing the necklace or holding the stone?

No comment

Say: You know that your friend has stolen someone's pen. The teacher asks you whether you know who stole the pen. You know who it was, but decide to remain silent.

Task question: 1. If you remain silent have you lied or told the truth (or something else)?

Task question: 2. Will the necklace allow you to remain silent?

Best friend

Say: You are really angry with your best friend. You think to yourself, 'I really hate you!' You know this will hurt your friend deeply. You say, 'I _____ you.' Because of the necklace, what you say is the truth.

Task question: Will you say, 'I hate you,' or will you say 'I love you' or something else?

Put both on!

Say: Is there anyone who would like to put both on?

Do: Return to the opening (uncontroversial) example and ask the first TQ again. Follow up with the following TQ:

Task question: What do you think you should say when you're holding both?

The liar's paradox

This famous paradox is from the ancient Greeks:

 A Cretan walks into a room and says 'All Cretans are liars!'

If the Cretan is saying what is true, then the Cretan is, being a Cretan, a liar. So, what he or she said must be a lie, and therefore false. It's a paradox because, if it is true then it is false! To do the liar's paradox with the class …

Say: All teachers are liars!

Task question: 1. What does it mean if what I just said is true?

Task question: 2. What does it mean if what I just said is false?

Links

Once Upon an If: The Promise Slippers

The If Machine: Goldfinger; The Shadow of the Pyramid

The Man on The Moon by Simon Bart Ram (**TQ:** Is he telling the truth?)

The Philosophy Shop: Tralse; Zeno's Parting Shot; Negative Nelly; The Accidental Confession; Happiness and Truth

Thoughtings: Puzzles and Paradoxes section

THE TELEKINETIC TEACHER

Thinking about causes, forces and magic

Precisely beause of the contrast between the two, magic is a great way to approach science enquiries. Together with the 'disappointing fake magic trick' device (see page 62), this session (or variations of) is useful with any discussion around science, causes and forces.

Equipment and preparation needed
- Have some magnets to hand
- Get hold of a piece of thin paper that is easy to move by blowing
- Get hold of a ring, such as a wedding ring, and an elastic band snapped once to form a single, discontinuous elastic band thread; rehearse the telekinetic 'magic' trick (see below)
- Get hold of some dominoes and a tall, thin item that is likely to fall over easily when knocked, such as the packaging box for a toothpaste tube

Key controversies
What makes things happen? Is a magnet's unique ability to move another object without touch a demonstration of a scientific anomaly? What exactly is the difference between magic and science?

Key concepts and vocabulary
Attraction/Repulsion | Movement
Causation | Push/Pull
Fields | Telekinesis
Force | Touch
Magnetism

Subject links
Magnets
Materials
Science (forces)

Key facilitation tool
Welcome assumptions

KEY FACILITATION TOOL

Welcome assumptions

It is easy to think that making assumptions is a bad thing, but this is not necessarily the case. First, we need to make some assumptions or else conversations wouldn't get off the ground. Sometimes it is good to keep an assumption in a question or statement that you are using to work with so that the children have something to react to. So, the question 'When is a dog not a dog?' (see 'The dog that meowed' on page 30) assumes that it is possible for a dog not to be a dog, but leaving this assumption in has two positive outcomes: 1. it encourages divergence and dialogue; 2. it invites the children to spot that there may be a contradiction. In short: leaving in assumptions can be good for critical thinking. But, two notes: first, make sure that you are *aware* of any assumptions that may be present in a question, and second – especially if it's your own question – make sure that you don't mind the children challenging it. So, if the question is 'How do you *know* that aliens exist?', this leaves in the assumption that they do. If this were something you didn't want the children to critically engage with, this would not be a good formulation of the question.

Do: Have the following definition ready but only reveal it, bit by bit if necessary, when the children identify the salient definition feature. If they know nothing about the word you may need to begin by providing a starting definition to which nuances can be added: *moving things without touching them.*

Definition of *telekinesis* (also *psychokinesis*)

… movement of physical objects by the power of the mind, carried out at a distance. From the Greek tele = 'distant' and 'kinesis' = motion

Longman's Dictionary of The English Language

Say: What, if anything, can you tell me about telekinesis? [Write the word up.]

Say: I shall now move some objects using the power of telekinesis.

Do: Perform each of the 'telekinetic tricks' to the class. After each trick say 'Ta-da!', then ask the following task question:

Task question: **1. Did I just do telekinesis?**

1. Say that you will move a piece of paper [hold it up] without touching it. Place a thin piece of paper on a desk in front of you, then blow on the paper so that it moves.

2. Say that you will switch the light on/off without moving from where you are standing. You may want to plan this one in advance. Point towards the switch, leave a dramatic pause and signal with your eyes to the teacher, or another adult in the room, to move over to the light switch and turn the light off.

3. Say that you will move an item [take the item – see below – and place it down in the right place] without touching it. Stand something up that's tall and thin and likely to fall over easily, such as the box of a toothpaste tube. Then issue instructions to class members to line up some dominoes leading to the item, and to set the dominoes off at the opposite end from the item so that the dominoes knock over the item.

4. Say that you will move a ring up an incline without touching it.

   a. For this trick take the ring and the elastic band (see 'Equipment needed', above) and thread the elastic band through the ring.

   b. Hold the elastic band with both hands, one holding either end.

   c. Hold one hand slightly higher than the other so that the band forms a not-too-steep diagonal line, and make sure that the lower of the two hands has plenty of excess elastic band concealed in the fist.

   d. Stretch the elastic band with the other hand as you hold it up to begin the trick, but do not show that you have stretched it.

e. The ring should now be at the bottom of the incline, resting against your hand.

f. Without moving either of your hands, slowly release (using your thumb) the concealed elastic band so that the ring travels upwards towards your other hand on the elastic band (the ring should stick to the band quite naturally). It will look as if the ring is moving 'telekinetically' up the band, though really it is being carried.

It's a simple trick to perform, and once you've mastered it (practise before you perform!) it looks great, especially if you add a little theatricality to it, such as really concentrating on the ring and straining your face and so on. There is a video in the online resources that accompany this book showing you how it's done!

5. Say that you will move a piece of metal without touching it. Take out your magnets and then move some magnetic metal, but also move one of the magnets with the other, both by attracting it and repelling it.

Do: After repeating TQ1 move to the next task question; again, only if necessary.

Task question: 2. Is magnetism magic?

Nested questions

- What is magnetism?
- What is magic?
- What is science?
- What is the difference between all three?
- Are there any similarities between them?
- What is movement?
- How do things move?
- Do all forms of movement have the same kind of cause?

EXTENSION ACTIVITY

Animus magnetism

Say: : In the early days of science, long before scientific method had been established, the 'natural philosophers' investigated the world by making generalisations about the world around them from observations they made. Here is an example of this that has been attributed, by later philosophers such as Aristotle, to Thales of Miletus (624–546 BCE):

- A soul has the power to move the body.
- A magnet has the power to move iron.
- Therefore, a magnet has a soul.

He also concluded from this argument that all things have souls.

Do: Present the argument attributed to Thales (see above), then critically engage the class with the following question: Do you agree with Thales? There are two parts to this: 1. Do they agree with the argument for why magnets have souls? and 2. Do they agree with his general claim that 'All things have souls'?

Magnetic doughnut

Place a doughnut (or similarly irresistible foodstuff) on a plate, and put it on the floor or on a nearby table. Watch the children be drawn 'magnetically' towards it. This can help the class draw distinctions between different meanings of 'attraction' and 'magnetism'.

Task question: **Is the doughnut magnetic?**

How is this so?

How is this so?
It is so, because it is so.
How is this not so?
It is not so, because it is not so.
How does this occur?
It occurs, because it occurs.
How does this not occur?
It does not occur, because it does not occur. From *The Book of Chuang Tzu*

Task question: **Why are things as they are?**

Nested questions

Are the claims that are made in this poem true? (For example: is it true that 'it is so because it is so'?)

• Does this poem provide good explanations for why things are as they are?

• If not, what would be a good explanation?

• What is an explanation?

Links

Once Upon an If: The Magician's Tricks – The Fire Stick
The If Machine: The Shadow of the Pyramid
The Philosophy Foundation website: Things Are Not Always What They Seem (free download)
The Philosophy Shop: What Goes Up …; The Broken Window
Thoughtings: The Law of Grabbity

HUMPTY DUMPTY

Thinking about words and meaning

The Adventures of Alice in Wonderland is a treasure-trove of starting places for philosophical (and other) discussions and enquiries. This and the next Thought Adventure serve as an introduction to how one might make use of the book more generally. Feel free to use this as a model for further enquires inspired by the Oxford mathematician and logician Charles Dodgson, aka the children's writer Lewis Carroll.

Equipment and preparation needed

• A copy of *Alice's Adventures in Wonderland* and *Through the Looking Glass and What Alice Found There* (I recommend *The Annotated Alice* edited by Martin Gardner – the annotations make for fascinating reading, revealing that much of the 'nonsense' has genuinely interesting logical/philosophical roots) – look at Chapter 6 of *Through the Looking Glass*, 'Humpty Dumpty', and Chapter 7 of *Alice's Adventures in Wonderland*, 'A Mad Tea-Party' (optional)

Key controversies

Is the connection between meaning and words arbitrary or intrinsic? Are there any rules for how to use meaning in words? Is it possible to have a 'private language' – a language only you speak?

Key concepts and vocabulary

Communication

Contextual meaning

Language

Meaning

Mutability of language

Naming

Private language

Rules

Stipulative meaning

Understanding

Words

Subject links

Literacy

Maths

Numeracy

Poetry

Key facilitation tool

Clarification opening-up strategy

KEY FACILITATION TOOL

Clarification opening-up strategy

'Would you mind saying what you mean by X?' (see 'Opening up' in Appendix 1) is useful here because it requires that someone say what they mean by a term. Once it is clear how someone is using a term, it is possible to evaluate their argument, whether or not they are using the term correctly, or as it is commonly used. So: if, when I use 'sausage' I mean 'three', then the following argument, though appearing nonsensical, is a good one:

• Two is greater than one.

• Sausage is greater than two.

• Therefore, sausage is greater than one.

Say: In the story *Alice's Adventures in Wonderland* and its sequel, *Through the Looking Glass*, we meet a curious little girl aged – she says, 'seven years and six months'. She enters a very strange, dream-like world where the usual rules and laws of the world don't seem to apply; a place where things get farther away the more you walk towards them, a place where there are potions and mushrooms that change your size, and a place where you can drown in your own tears.
In the second story, *Through the Looking Glass*, Alice attempts to buy an egg from a shopkeeper. The shopkeeper says, 'I never put things into people's hands – that would never do – you must get it for yourself.' Whereupon she takes the egg and places it on a shelf at the far end of the shop. As Alice makes her way towards the egg, at first it seems to get further away but then …

> *The egg only got larger and larger and more human: when she had come within a few yards of it, she saw that it had eyes and a nose and mouth: and, when she had come close to it, she saw clearly that it was _____/_____. [Leave out who it is, for them to fill in. If the class need a little more, then keep reading.] He was sitting with his legs crossed on the top of a high wall – such a narrow one that Alice quite wondered how he could keep his balance … 'And how exactly like an egg he is!' she said aloud.*

From *Through the Looking Glass* by Lewis Carroll

ENQUIRY 1

Task question: **What is this character's name? (The character's name is *Humpty Dumpty*, of course, but only tell the class if necessary.)**

Nested questions

- If you know who it is, how do you know?
- Alice says that she is as certain that he is Humpty Dumpty as if his name were written all over his face. Why is this?
- Alice also says that 'It can't be anybody else!' Is she right?
- Is it possible to know someone's name before they tell you, just from how they look?
- Do people look like their names?
- Do any people look like they have the wrong name? If so, what would be a better name? How would you decide?

See extension activity for Enquiry 1 below.

ENQUIRY 2: DIALOGUE 1

Do: Either read out to your class the short dialogues below, adapted from the chapter 'Humpty Dumpty' in *Through the Looking Glass* or, better still, have members of the class read/act them out. Then ask the accompanying task question.

Humpty: What is your name?
Alice: My name is Alice.
Humpty: What does it mean?
Alice: *Must* a name mean something?
Humpty: Of course it must! *My* name means the shape I am.

Does a name have to mean something?

Nested questions

- Does your name mean something?
- Does 'Humpty Dumpty' mean 'the shape he is'?
- What does 'Humpty Dumpty' mean, if anything?

See extension activity for Enquiry 2 below.

ENQUIRY 3: DIALOGUE 2

Humpty: How old did you say you were?

Alice: Seven years and six months.

Humpty: Wrong! You never said a word like it.

Alice: I thought you meant 'How old are you?'

Humpty: If I'd meant that, I'd have said it.

Task question: 1. Do we always say what we mean?

Task question: 2. Do we always mean what we say?

Task question: 3. Is saying what you mean the same as meaning what you say?

See the extension activity for Enquiry 3, 'The Mad Tea-Party'.

EXTENSION ACTIVITY

Game: It can't be anybody else! – extension activity for Enquiry 1. ('It can't be anybody else' are the words Alice exclaims when she infers that the character sitting on the wall must be Humpty Dumpty.)

1) Explain that the class have to guess who you are describing and that it will be someone in the class. Start with yourself.
2) Say, 'The person is [insert your gender. E.g. In my case, Male].' Take guesses.
3) Say, 'The person was born before [insert present year. E.g. 2015].' Take guesses.
4) Say, 'The person is [insert your height. E.g. 5'9"].' Take guesses.
5) Say, 'The person is [insert a distinguishing feature of yourself. E.g. In my case grey!].' Take guesses.
6) Questions:
- Was it easy to guess with the first clue? Why or why not?
- Was it easier to guess with any of the other clues? Which ones, and why?

1) Play the game *It can't be anybody else!*

    ☐ One child has to get the rest of the class to guess someone else in the room with only a description.

    ☐ They are only allowed to say three things about the person.

    ☐ They should take only one guess after each stage.

    ☐ If someone gets it right after the first guess the child gets 3 points, they get 2 points if a correct guess comes after the second bit of information and they get only 1 point after the third.

Name the ball – extension activity for Enquiry 2

1) Have the class name the talk-ball.

2) Stipulate that it must be completely original; it cannot be a name or word already in use. (One of my classes had 'Chamallywalla'!)

3) Write up a few suggestions that meet the stipulations then have the children vote on one. The name they vote on becomes the new name for the talk ball.

Task question: **Is [insert new name] a name? Does it mean anything?**

Nested questions

• Where do names come from?

• How do names work?

• Can anyone invent a name?

• What is a name?

• How are names different from descriptions? (See the game *It can't be anybody else!* Above)

The Mad Tea-Party – extension activity for Enquiry 3

Here's a relevant extract, to be read to the class either by you or another class-member, from an earlier chapter, 'A Mad Tea-Party', from the earlier story *Alice's Adventures in Wonderland*:

'Do you mean that you think you can find the answer to it ['it' here is a riddle: Why is a raven like a writing desk?]?' said the March Hare.

'Exactly so,' said Alice.

'Then you should say what you mean,' the March Hare went on.

'I do,' Alice hastily replied; 'at least - at least I mean what I say - that's the same thing, you know.'

'Not the same thing a bit!' said the Hatter. 'Why, you might just as well say that 'I see what I eat' is the same as 'I eat what I see'!'

'You might just as well say,' added the March Hare, 'that 'I like what I get' is the same thing as 'I get what I like'!'

'You might just as well say,' added the Dormouse, which seemed to be talking in its sleep, 'that 'I breathe when I sleep' is the same thing as 'I sleep when I breathe'!'

'It is the same thing with you,' said the Hatter, and here the conversation dropped and the party sat silent for a minute.

1) Is saying what you mean the same as meaning what you say?
2) Is 'I see what I eat' the same as 'I eat what I see'?
3) Is 'I like what I get' the same as 'I get what I like'?
4) Is 'I breathe when I sleep' the same as 'I sleep when I breathe'?

Consider the following examples:

Nisha: Are you coming out to play tonight?
Sean: I have homework to do.

Task questions:

- What did Sean *say*?
- What did Sean *mean*?
- Did Sean say what he meant?
- Did Sean mean what he said?

Sue: 'But Miss, I ain't doin' nuffink!'

Questions:
- Did Sue say what she meant?
- Did Sue mean what she said?

Links

The If Machine: Goldfinger, The Meaning of Ant Life, The Chair

The If Odyssey: Clouded, Winged Words

Once Upon an If: The Cat That Barked, The Boy With No Name, It, Stories in Verse

The Philosophy Shop: Language and Meaning or What can be said about what there is, Wondering about Wonderland

Thoughtings: Word Wonders, Poems to Do, Number Wonders, Puzzles and Paradoxes

HUMPTY-DUMPTYING

Thinking about meaning and words

Believe it or not, humptydumptying is a thing: one humptydumpties when one changes the meaning of a word from its common usuage to suit one's purposes. See this session to see why this word means what it means. Or does it?

Equipment and preparation needed
• A talk ball

Key controversies
Is it possible to have a private language?

Subject links
Languages
Literacy

Key concepts and vocabulary

Communication	Mutability of language	Stipulative meaning
Contextual meaning	Naming	Understanding
Language	Private language	Words
Meaning	Rules	

Do: Read out or have the children perform the following dialogue from Chapter 6 of *Through The Looking Glass*, 'Humpty Dumpty':

Say: :

Alice: I don't know what you mean by 'glory'.

Humpty: Of course you don't – till I tell you. I meant: 'there's a nice knock-down argument for you!'

Alice: But 'glory' doesn't mean 'a nice knock-down argument'.

Humpty: When I use a word it means just what I choose it to mean – no more or less.

Alice: The question is whether you can make words mean so many different things.

Humpty: The question is which is to be master, that's all.

Task question: Can a word mean just what you choose it to mean?

Nested questions
• Can we decide the meaning of words?
• How is the meaning of a word decided?
• Do meanings of words change?

Say: Today we will run the discussion as follows: I will pass the ball to a girl to start, then, when she has finished, she will pass the ball to a boy who hasn't spoken yet. When he has finished, he will pass the ball to a girl who hasn't spoken yet and we will carry on like that.

Do: Once the question has been asked and the class have been given some talk time, choose a girl – maybe using a random selection method (see page 101) – who wants to start, then allow them to follow the procedure described above. After each contribution say: 'Thank you, now could you pass the ball to a girl/boy who has not yet spoken! Thank you.' Repeat this after every contribution then…

At some point, begin to 'humptydumpty-around' with some of the key words. Do this gradually, with no explanation or warning about what you are doing, so that, for instance:

- 'ball' becomes 'sausage'
- 'girl' = 'tree',
- 'boy' = 'clock'
- 'talk' = 'fish'

- Throw a few curve balls too, such as replacing 'pass', not with another verb-word but with a noun-word, such as 'mountain', or by replacing one of the 'humptydumpty' words with a new word *each time* so that it's not consistent (if you can manage it!). You could even introduce a completely new word that you have made up on the spot such as 'thrump' for 'guess'. In short: have fun!

- The aim of this activity is to do the very thing they are discussing – change the meaning of words in a variety of different ways. If the children get confused at what you are doing, repeat the instruction with a completely straight face (if you can manage it!) until they perform the correct action. Because of the easily discernible context, most of the classes I have done this with understand and barely notice the irony.

- You may want to ask them what it is they think you've been doing, if they're not already commenting.

Task question: **Does what I have been doing mean that we *can* choose what words mean?**

Extension activities:

Have the children invent their own languages. You may want to limit them to a 'dictionary' of 20 words and you may want to give them some basic structures to work with such as 'to have', 'to be', 'to go' and 'to do'. Have them decide whether they will do this on their own or in pairs or groups by asking the following task question:

Task question: **Can you do this task on your own or do you need to do this in pairs or groups?**

Nested questions

- What is a language?
- How do languages work?
- What is a language for?
- Can you have a private language; a language only you speak?

Links

Knuffle Bunny by Mo Willems (TQ: Does Trixie Talk?)

The If Machine: Goldfinger; The Meaning of Ant Life; The Chair

The If Odyssey: Clouded; Winged Words

Once Upon an If: The Cat That Barked; The Boy With No Name; It; Stories in Verse

The Philosophy Shop: Language and Meaning or What can be said about what there is; Wondering about Wonderland

Thoughtings: Word Wonders; Poems to Do; Number Wonders; Puzzles and Paradoxes

MIRRORED

Thinking about others

This session invites the children to reflect (sorry!) on the moral of a story by inviting them to think of their own. This is another of the sessions that allows children to critically engage with the interpretation of stories. Perfect also as a creative writing activity.

Equipment and preparation needed
• Learn the story to tell (optional)

Subject links
Literacy
PSHE

Key controversies
To what extent can we understand someone else?

Key facilitation tool
Antithetical response detector

Key concepts and vocabulary
Empathy   Perspective
Hate   Point of view
Identity   Understanding
Other

KEY FACILITATION TOOL

Antithetical response detector

In order to find controversy in a class or group it can sometimes be useful to identify the person in the room, if there is such a person, who thinks antithetically, rather than simply passing the ball and hoping someone will have something divergent to say. So, if the first speaker thinks 'X' (for example that 'the ship is the same ship') then, occasionally, it can be fruitful to ask, 'Is there anyone who thinks "not X"?' (In this case, that 'the ship is not the same ship'.) And even if there's just *one* person who thinks 'not X', it might be enough to get the conversation going – to find the 'bite point' in the discussion. (See 'The imaginary disagreer' on page 122 for what to do if there's no one who thinks antithetically, and 'Response detectors' in Appendix 1.)

Do: Read or tell the following opening to a story.

Say: *Fyodor and Ivan were neighbouring farmers. Fyodor hated Ivan. Ivan hated Fyodor. They hated each other. Fyodor hated the way Ivan ate with his mouth open. Ivan hated the way Fyodor hummed to himself. Fyodor hated the way Ivan looked when he thought he was right and Ivan hated the way Fyodor looked when he thought Ivan was right. And there were plenty more things besides that they each hated about the other.*

This week they hated each other even more than usual. Ivan had started to plough a piece of land that he thought belonged to neither of them but when Fyodor found out, he claimed that the land was his. It was difficult to tell exactly who it belonged to.

After Ivan had ploughed the land Fyodor sowed it. Then Ivan released a huge flock of birds that ate all the seeds. Then Ivan sowed it with his own seeds. Then Fyodor released a large mischief of mice to eat all of Ivan's seeds, then he ploughed the land. Fyodor ploughed it again! Then Ivan! Then Fyodor … until all the ploughing brought something up out of the belly of the land and into their lives; something that would change them forever.

It was Fyodor that noticed it first. What looked like a wooden casket was jutting up through the soil. United for a moment by mutual curiosity, without consulting each other, they worked together to uncover the mysterious artefact. When they had dug it up, they found that it was a coffin. Silently and in perfect synchronisation, they opened it. Inside were the remains of a person; they could not tell whether it was a man or a woman as all that was left were the mildew-covered bones of a skeleton. But in each bony hand the skeleton held a small mirror. Because there were two mirrors, and perhaps because they were both wide-eyed with wonder, Ivan and Fyodor took only one, each taking the one nearest him. Instinctively, they held the mirrors up and peered inside. Both screamed, 'Aaaaagggghhh!'

[Ask the audience what it is they think Ivan and Fyodor saw when they looked in the mirrors.]

What they saw when they looked in the mirrors filled them both with terror. They dropped the mirrors and ran back to their respective houses. What they had seen was not their own reflection staring back at them but that of the other.

Task question: **What is going to happen?**

Write your own moral

This should be treated as a story-writing exercise in which the children write their own ending with their own moral. Before writing anything though, they should be given the opportunity to explore what a moral of a story is and what they think should happen; in other words, what do they think the story should teach the reader?

1. Follow the PaRDeS procedure (see Appendix 2) but with a small alteration. Instead of asking the following question for the moral level: 'What do we learn from this story?' the question will be:
   'What do you think a reader should learn from this story?'

2. Once the children have discussed this question have them write down the moral of their story.
   For example, 'It should teach that hate only leads to unhappiness.'

3. Then have them write their stories so that their stories contain their morals.

4. A follow-up discussion could be had about whether their stories successfully teach the moral they wrote down.

5. A further follow-up discussion could be had about whether the morals they wrote down are good morals.

Here are two examples I have had from some Year 4 (age eight) children:

• They have to learn to be nice to each other before they return to themselves.

• They learn that they are in fact brothers and the skeleton was once their father.

(A discussion was had about whether these were, in fact, both morals, leading to a discussion about what a 'moral of a story' is.)

EXTENSION ACTIVITY

A new Ceebie story

Write an extension story to 'The Ceebie Stories' (see page 58, and *The If Machine*) in which Jack's dad makes another CB1000, just like the first, identical in every detail and complete with memories.

Task question: Is there now more than one Ceebie?

You could play around with this idea:

• What if the new Ceebie was identical in every way except that Jack's dad had made the new one look like a girl?

• What if Jack's dad linked up the two Ceebies by wireless connection so that the two Ceebies could access the contents of each other's computer 'brains'?

Links

Once Upon an If: Water People; The Square That Didn't Fit In; The Two Sindbads (**TQ:** Can a rich person understand a poor person?); The Pit and the Old Man of the Sea (**TQ:** Are Sindbad's acts of killing in any way understandable?)

The If Machine: The Prince and the Pig; Billy Bash (another unfinished story to try out the story-writing exercise described above with); Yous On Another Planet; Where Are You?

The If Odyssey: The Concealer

The Philosophy Shop: Metaphysics: Personal Identity, especially The Copy Machine

Thoughtings: 'You, Me, Aliens and Others', especially Who's That?

ART DETECTIVES

Thinking about standards of beauty

This session is great for teaching, or having the children teach themselves, the fact/value distinction (usually made by the children as 'fact/opinion' distinction). However, this session can also allow classes (and teachers) to go deeper, to consider whether there are any grounds for thinking that beauty is something other than subjective (a matter of opinion): could it be inter-subjective (a matter of opinion but shared) or even objective (e.g. part of the world, like fossils).

Equipment and preparation needed

- You will need up to eight portrait pictures (e.g. two Rubens portraits, a Titian and a Memling for the first part; a Rubens, a Picasso, a grotesque and an abstract for the second)
- A couple of music stands to prop the pictures up
- Something that can be used as 'the beauty detector'; a hand-held machine of some kind – you could 'make' one (optional)

Key controversies

Is beauty in the eye of the beholder? Can reasons be given for why something is beautiful? Can there be a standard or standards of beauty?

Key concepts and vocabulary

Beauty   Style
Objective   Subjective
Realism   Ugliness

Subject links

Art
Portraits

Key facilitation tool

Provoke (see below and page 6)

KEY FACILITATION TOOL

Provoke

I think this should be done sparingly in the classroom, but when done right, provoking a response can be a very effective catalyst to lively discussion. If you feel uncomfortable playing Devil's advocate, you could always insert 'If I were to say …' just before the provocative statement. I avoid this technique if I suspect I'm using it to share my own opinions. It's better if you can draw the reason for using it from somewhere other than your own views. In this case, it's drawn from the children themselves, as in the example below. (See also 'Here's a thought' on page 4.)

STYLE DETECTIVES

Do: For the first activity, put up the four portraits. Make sure you include two portraits by the same painter. On the board behind each picture write a corresponding number: 1, 2, 3 and 4, so the children can easily refer to the pictures.

Say: I have a task for you. The task is to identify which two of these four paintings are by the same painter.

Do: In a class of 30 invite them up in groups of about five or six. Once this is done, spend a few minutes allowing the children to say which two paintings are by the same painter and insist on them saying *why* they think what they think. Make a tally of choices on the board for later. Once this is done, reveal who painted which painting by explaining their dates and so on.

BEAUTY DETECTIVES

Do: Change the paintings. I usually keep one Rubens up and add a Picasso, a grotesque and an abstract painting by way of contrast.

Say: This time the task is to identify the most beautiful painting.

Do: Repeat the procedure as above if necessary. Remember to insist that the children say *why* they have chosen the picture they have. You could follow this with the following task question:

Task question: **How can we decide, if at all, which is the most beautiful picture?**

Or you could …

Say: Shall I tell you the answer?

This should be enough to get some hands of protest up in the air! You may be worried about having to give one if you say this, so here's a strategy if you find yourself in that position (if someone says 'But that's just your opinion' you can confidently reply that it's not!):

Say: Here's an answer [simply look at the tally on the board and select the one with the most votes]: the most beautiful picture is [insert picture with the most votes].

Do: Of course, you should reveal how you got 'the answer' eventually, but maybe not straight away. It should lead to a good enquiry:

Task question: **Can a vote decide which picture is the most beautiful?**

Nested questions

- Can beauty be decided by a majority?
- Can beauty be decided by anything? If so, what?
- Does beauty exist?
- Is beauty in the eye of the beholder?
- Is beauty anywhere?
- Are there things that cause beauty?
- Are there things that cause the responses that make us say that 'X is beautiful'? If so, is that the same as saying that some things are beautiful?

EXTENSION ACTIVITY

Ugly detectives

You could follow the same procedure described in 'Beauty detectives', making sure to include an 'ugly' picture such as *The Ugly Duchess* by Matsys (1466–1530) and setting the following task: *To find the ugliest painting*. Thanks to Richard Anthone for this inversion of the idea.

THE BEAUTY DETECTOR

Say: This is a machine that has been designed to detect the most beautiful object. David is a scientist who has made a machine that detects beautiful things. He points it at things and it tells him how beautiful any object is.

Do: (You could do this using your phone, pretending that you have an app that detects beautiful things like Shazam detects songs.)

The question is …

Task question: What sort of thing would David's 'beauty detector' detect in the objects you point it at?

Could it use, as its data …

- The opinions of experts? (**TQ:** Could an expert decide? If so, then how?)
- The opinions of the many? (**TQ:** Could you decide with a vote? See above.)
- The presence of colour?
- Balance between different parts?
- How much effort has been put in?
- Or some other fact …?
- Does it capture an essence?

Links

Once Upon an If: The Valley of the Diamonds

Philosophy For Young Children: Aesthetics: beauty, pictures and stories

Plato Was Wrong!: 'What is Art?'

The If Machine: The Chair; The Meaning of Ant Life

The If Odyssey: The War; The Battle ('moral relativism'); Dinner Guests (+ online supplement)

The Philosophy Shop: Value: Aesthetics; The Goodness Detector; Metaphysics: Fiction

Thoughtings: Are Things Always What They Seem To Us To Be?; Colour; Bite; Lines

DIOGENES AND ALEXANDER

Thinking about the good life

With this session, invite the children to consider one of the Ancient Greek's favourite philosophical questions: what is a good life? Though probably apocryphal, this story asks us to consider the relationship between happiness and freedom. As, Solon, the Athenian lawgiver said, 'Let no man be called happy until he is dead.' What could that mean?!

Equipment and preparation needed
- Familiarise yourself with the PaRDeS method described in Appendix 2
- Learn the story to tell (optional)

Subject links
Art

Key controversies
How can you have a happy life if you have no wealth or possessions?

Key facilitation tool
Instant dramatisation (see page 153)

Key concepts and vocabulary
Freedom
Happiness
Independence

Moral duty
Responsibility
Values

A little philosophy

The Cynics were members of one of the schools of philosophical thinking that grew out of the Hellenistic period: that period of Greek culture that spread through Europe after Alexander the Great's rise to power. The others were the Stoics (see page 24), the Sceptics and the Epicureans, all of which were said to have been inspired, in one way or another, by Socrates. The names of all these schools have since been adopted by users of the English language (and others) to mean something slightly different from their philosophical origins. The key idea behind Cynicism was to keep life simple, good and true. This meant that Cynics eschewed social convention and preferred a direct, brutally honest way of being.

Say: To give you an idea of how the early Greek philosophers in this story are linked, here's a quick rundown: Socrates (c. 470–399 BCE) was the teacher of Plato; Plato was the teacher of Aristotle; Aristotle was the teacher of Alexander the Great who was, as you will find out, a contemporary of Diogenes.

This story is about two people, each of whom believed themselves to have the best life; each of them believed himself to be free. They are Diogenes of Sinope and Alexander the Great.

Do: Insert here any further biographical details about Alexander that you like or that you need.

Say: *Alexander was so powerful he could do whatever he wanted. He would never be punished because there was simply no authority greater than him. If he wanted something, he would have it; if he wanted someone killed, it would be done; if a mountain was in the way of his marching army it would be moved by his slaves, rock by rock. Diogenes had no possessions, but he would say that he was able to have whatever he wanted, too. This was because he only wanted what he needed and what was good. If he was hungry, he would eat some bread and water, if he wanted to be comfortable, he would stand out of the sun's glare or shelter from the rain, if he wanted to say something, he would say it.*

This is the story of how Alexander the Great and Diogenes met, and it begins not with Diogenes or Alexander, but with Socrates.

It is said that Socrates one day visited the many stalls in the Agora – or marketplace – of Athens. Having taken one look at all the things on sale there he was said to have declared: 'Look at all these things I don't need!'

Some time later, a man called Diogenes lived in a large house filled with beautiful things. He was very rich and was waited on by many slaves, but Diogenes was unhappy. There were always people asking him for money, there were things to be done, buildings to be mended and slaves to look after. He never seemed to have any time to himself to think, which was one thing Diogenes liked to do very much.

One day Diogenes saw a dog loose on the street doing exactly what it wanted to do when it wanted to do it. He noticed that, though the dog owned nothing, it seemed very happy and free. He thought that maybe it was because the dog owned nothing that the dog was happy and free. He recalled the story of Socrates in the Agora that he had been told as a child. Taking a look at his house, his riches and his servants, he thought to himself: 'I don't need any of this stuff. In fact,' he thought, 'I think I'd be better off without it.' So, Diogenes decided to leave his house and his possessions behind. He freed his slaves and set off into the big, wide world. Finally, he believed he was free.

Task question: **Is Diogenes happy and free?**

Nested questions
- What is it to be free?
- What is it to be happy?
- Is the dog free?

Say: *Eventually, Diogenes found his way to Athens and he became a famous citizen of the city. He had no great house or slaves; all he had was a cloak, a stick, a cup and a barrel for shelter that could be found just outside the city walls. Every day, followers and well-wishers would bring him bread, cheese, water and fruit; just enough to sustain him. He became so famous that word of his teachings and his ideas reached the most powerful man in the Mediterranean world: Alexander the Great. Alexander was the emperor of the largest empire that had ever existed up to that time. Although Alexander was a great military leader he had in his youth – as you'll recall – been taught by the philosopher Aristotle.*

Those that followed the teachings of Diogenes became known as 'Cynics', which came from the Greek for 'dog', perhaps because of the inspiration Diogenes had received from the dog he had seen in the street that day. Because of the great respect Alexander had for the strange old man outside the walls of Athens, he desired to visit Diogenes and pay his respects. So he travelled all the way to Athens. The people of Athens heard of his approach and prepared a lavish welcome for the famous Emperor, with lots of expensive food and wine for him and his men to feast upon, and many slaves to wait upon him. But when he arrived, Alexander wasn't interested in their grand gestures; he went straight to Diogenes' barrel and said to him 'I am Alexander the Great, the most powerful man in all the world, and out of respect for your teachings I would like to offer you anything you desire. Name it, and it shall be yours.'

Diogenes looked up at Alexander and said, 'There is one thing you can do for me.' To which Alexander said, 'Name it.'

'Could you move a little to the left,' said Diogenes, waving his hand to the left side, 'because you are blocking out the sun.'

One of Alexander's guards, unused to such insolence before his leader, raised his spear to execute Diogenes. Alexander lifted his hand to stop the guard, and said, 'Do not harm this man, for truly, if I were not Alexander, I would wish to be Diogenes.'

Hermeneutic question: What did Alexander the Great mean when he said:
'… truly, if I were not Alexander, I would wish to be Diogenes'?

Task question: Which one of them has the best life?

Nested questions

- What is the best life?
- Do you think that you would be happier with more stuff, or less stuff?
- What did Socrates mean when he said 'Look at all these things I don't need'?
- What do you need to be happy?
- Do you think you would be more free/happy with just a cloak, a stick, a cup and a barrel, or less free/happy?
- What is freedom?
- What is happiness?
- If you had to choose, would you be Alexander the Great or Diogenes the Cynic? Why?
- Is your personal happiness important, or are there more important things?
- Who, if anyone, would you rather be?

More interpretation

Try this story with the PaRDeS method, adapting as necessary (see Appendix 2).

'I am the law.'

This phrase comes from comic book character Judge Dredd, but could easily have been said by someone like Alexander the Great. You could take this aspect of the story further by returning to the following passage in the story:

> *Alexander was so powerful he could do whatever he wanted. He would never be punished because there was simply no authority greater than him. If he wanted something, he would have it; if he wanted someone killed, it would be done; if a mountain was in the way of his marching army it would be moved by his slaves, rock by rock.*

Task question: **Can Alexander do whatever he wants?**

Nested questions

- What, if anything, can he not do?
- Is there anything that he should not do?
- If there is no one to stop you doing something is there any reason to refrain from doing bad things?
- What would a religious person say in answer to the first Nested question?
- What would a morally good person say in answer to the first Nested question?
- What would your mother say in answer to the first Nested question?

Links

Once Upon an If: The Promise Slippers; The Fair Well; The Magic Crown; The Two Sindbads; The Valley of the Diamonds; The Saddle; The Pit; The Old Man of the Sea

Philosophy for Young Children: Chapters 1–4

Plato Was Wrong!: Chapters 6 and 7

The If Machine: The Meaning of Ant Life; Republic Island; The Ring of Gyges; The Prince and The Pig; The Happy Prisoner

The If Odyssey: Happiness and Forgetting; Captain or Crew?; Choices

The Philosophy Shop: Value: Politics; Value: Ethics

Thoughtings: Love, Goodness and Happiness

Instant dramatisation

When you have stories to read that have details a class may find difficult to follow, the first tip is to tell the story in a lively way; simply reading a story from a page is a lot less likely to come across well to an audience. Some story details challenge even a good storyteller, however. In which case, enlist the class to help tell the story. Ask for volunteers to act out the story as you tell it. Point to a class member (one who has expressed a wish to participate) as you introduce new characters. Their job is to act out the scene you describe (with no words; it's very distracting if the children talk). As new characters are introduced, point to other volunteers. You may find that more students want to volunteer as you go on, so remember to keep finding out who wants to join in. When the class see the events of the story 'happen' before them, you will find that they follow the details of the story more easily.

Definitely/Maybe

This is a strategy developed by my colleague, TPF specialist Steven Hoggins, for use with very young children (Early Years), though it can be used with older children too. In order to encourage more clarity from the children he will often ask them if they think something 'definitely', 'definitely not' or 'maybe'. So, for example, 'Is it *definitely* money?' (he holds his thumb up while saying this), 'Is it *definitely* not money?' (he holds his thumb down while saying this), then he says, 'Or is it *maybe* money?' Then he 'opens them up' (see 'Open up' in Appendix 1): 'Can you say why?' You can vary this strategy with more sophisticated words for older children, such as, 'Do you think it *could* be? … Do you think it *can't* be? …' ('Definitely can't? Maybe can't?'), 'Do you think it *must* be?' and so on.

MONEY, MONEY, MONEY

Thinking about the value of currency

Like numbers or the self, money is one of those things where we all think we know what it is until we stop to think about it. This session forms a good extension activity to 'Republic Island' in The If Machine or 'Sindbad and The Valley of The Diamonds' in Once Upon an If.

Equipment and preparation needed

- A five-pound note
- Some pieces of paper about the same size as a five- or ten-pound note
- Some toy money (optional)

Subject links

Geography
History
PSHE

Key controversies

Is money valuable in itself? What does money represent?

Key facilitation tool

Definitely/maybe (see page 153)

Key concepts and vocabulary

Confidence	Money
Currency	Trade
Instrumental	Value
Intrinsic	

Do: Place a real five-pound note on the floor, a piece of paper with £5 written on it and, if you have it, a toy five-pound note. Then ask the following task question:

Task question: Are these pieces of paper worth the same?

Nested questions

- If not, why are they not worth the same?
- What gives money its worth?
- Is money just a piece of paper?
- What is money?

Do: This time, place two pieces of paper on the floor, one with '5' written on it and the other with '10' written on it. Ask the following task question:

Nested questions

- If not, why are they not worth the same?
- What gives money its worth?
- Is money just a piece of paper?
- What is money?

EXTENSION ACTIVITY

Desert island

Say: Imagine that all of you – that is the whole class – are stranded on a desert island. You have learned to survive on the island and have set up your own community, you have built homes and farms, and some of you have begun to trade. One of you has suggested that you create your own currency – your own money.

Task question: ▶ **How would you make your own money?**

Nested questions

- What makes money work?
- What makes money valuable?
- What is needed for you to be able to have money on your island?
- Do you just need paper with numbers written on?

Links

Once Upon an If: Valley of the Diamonds; The Saddle

The If Machine: Republic Island; The Meaning of Ant Life

The If Odyssey: Winged Words

The Philosophy Shop: Language and Meaning; Value: Aesthetics

Thoughtings: Asteroid; Lines; How Long is a String of Letters?; Order; Is There Something In It?; Invisible Punctuation

THE HIDING BOX

Thinking about a world without ...

This evocative session provides you – the teacher – with a general device ('What would the world be like with/without X?') that can be used again and again, starting with oranges and moving to any other appropriate noun, or abstract noun, such as love, money, death or evil.

Equipment and preparation needed

- A non-transparent box with a lid
- An orange, placed inside the box before the session so that the children do not know that it is there
- A piece of folded paper also placed in the box

Key controversies

What could possibly *not be*? Is there anything that *isn't*, that *could* have been? ... Or is this a nonsense?

Key concepts and vocabulary

'What if ...?'   Reference
Conditional sentences   Un-referred-to entities
Counterfactuals   Words
Hypothetical thinking

Subject links

Literacy (counterfactual thinking)
PSHE

Key facilitation tool

A world without see below

Say: I want you to imagine that this story really happened to you!

One day, a while ago, you moved house. Imagine that the house you moved into was an old house ...

Before all the furniture is moved in, you decide to run around the space the house is full of, as much as you can before all the furniture fills it up. You notice how rooms and houses have a special sound when they're empty.

Eventually you find a door that leads down into a dark cellar. Do you go down into the cellar? You decide to investigate. There's a light switch that dimly lights the stairway down into the cellar. After exploring the cellar thoroughly you find a small hole behind a loose brick in the wall by the floor in a hidden corner. You remove the brick and, pressing the side of your face against the cold cellar floor, you peer inside. It smells musty and damp. In the darkness you just see the side of something metal hidden inside the hole. Do you reach inside to retrieve the item you've spied? Your curiosity gets the better of you and you reach in and pull out a box. It's old and rusty.

Do: Take out the box you've prepared and hold it before you, then open the box.

Say: You open the box and are surprised to see two things inside it: something you've never seen before and a piece of folded paper. The thing inside that you've never seen before is orange and looks like some kind of fruit. It is round and has lots of little dimples on it.

Do: Reach in and take out the orange.

Say: 'Wow!' you say. 'It's an orange!' That's funny, because when it was in the box you didn't know what it was, but now that it's out of the box it's clearly an orange.

Do: Put it back in the box.

Say: 'What's that?! What a strange looking fruit!' you think.

Do: Take it out once more.

KEY FACILITATION TOOL

A world without …

A 'counterfactual' is a factual account of the world where the facts involved include facts that are other than how the world actually is. Counterfactuality provides us with a general tool that can be used again and again in many different teaching and learning situations. Simply take this question structure: 'What would the world be like without X(s)?' and add anything in place of X such as numbers, love, money, school or even teachers! You can invert this too: 'What would the world be like with X(s)?' The X could be anything from an 'incredible shrinking machine' to a necklace that makes you tell the truth.

Say: Then you have an idea. You decide to see if the folded piece of paper will have any answers. So you take out the paper, unfold it and read what's written on it:

 'This is a magical box,' it reads. 'It is a box of hiding. Anything that is placed in the box, either physically placed, or written as a word on a piece of paper, will no longer exist in the world.'

Say: So, now you understand what happens when you place the orange in the box and why you don't know what it is when it's in there. Because while it's in the box it doesn't exist!

Do: Place the orange in the box and then ask the following task question:

Task question: **What would the world be like without oranges?**

Nested questions
- Are oranges important?
- If there were no oranges can you think of anything else there wouldn't be? (Marmalade, for example.)
- What impact would having no oranges in the world have?
- Would you be worse off without the flavour of oranges?
- If you don't like oranges would it be better if there were no oranges?

Fill the box

Have the children write on a piece of paper something they would like to put into the box. Disallow other people or anything personal that would upset other students. Collect their entries by going around the class and having the students put their piece of paper into the hiding box. Like the anonymity exercise (see page 6) you now have the opportunity to go through the entries and to not make use of those entries that, for whatever reason, are inappropriate. Lay out the remaining entries on the floor as stimuli to discussion. Interestingly, every time I have done this – without exception – the X that has got the most entries is 'money'. The question 'What would the world be like without money?' also makes for an excellent discussion point and can be used with the 'money' session (see page 156) very effectively. This exercise is not only limited to this particular session; look out for other opportunities to use the hiding box exercise.

The Book of Everything and The Reality Glasses

(See pages 43 and 119.)

The Book:

Say: Make a list, if possible, of five things that don't exist but that could have existed.

Task question: **Would the list of 'things that don't exist but could have existed' be in the Book of Everything?**

The glasses:

Task question: **1. If you were to put on the reality glasses, would you see things that don't exist but could have?**

Task question: **2. Would you see possibilities that haven't been realised?**

Links

Once Upon an If: Once Upon an If (parts 1 and 2)
The If Machine: The Little Old Shop of Curiosities
The If Odyssey: Under The World; The Horror of The Rocks
Thoughtings: Possible World; The Stone; Impossibling; More Impossiblings

APPENDIX 1:
THINKING ABOUT FACILITATING IDEA-DIVERSITY

This is possibly the most important section in the book. The key to a good discussion is controversy, and controversy begins with a stimulus and/or a question that is contentious or leads to contention. But that is not always enough; you also need diversity of ideas within the group for the controversy to be understood *as such* by the group. The sessions in this book will give you the stimuli you need, but getting a good discussion going will be down to you. Here are some hints and tips to assist you in helping a good discussion along by encouraging diversity without having to do the all-too-common 'Devil's advocate' moves.

Open/Closed questions

Use grammatically closed questions ('So, is it a number?'), but conceptually open questions (the question behind this is 'What is a number?'). Closed questions require students to respond with 'yes'/'no' answers or short answers such as 'not free'. By posing questions in this binary form it encourages students to take a position and thereby enter into a dialectical relationship with the question and with each other (I think 'yes' but he thinks 'no'). It may surprise you to find out that by posing questions in binary form it actually encourages the students to challenge the posing of the problem in binary terms. They do so when they start to say things like, 'I think *both* …', 'I don't think "yes" *or* "no" …', '*In a way* "yes" and *in a way* "no" …', and so on. This kind of language implies that the concepts are more nuanced than the original question seemed to suggest and that, perhaps, distinctions need to be drawn.

Open up

When you use closed questions, just remember to open them up again. Here are the classic opening-up questions:

- **Justify:** 'Can you say *why* you think that?'
- **Clarify:** 'Can you say what you *mean* by X?'
- **Elicit:** 'Can you say *more* about that?'
- **Exemplify:** 'Can you give an *example* of that?'
- **Test for implications or entailments:** 'Can you say what that *tells* us about …?' or 'What do you think that means?'
- **Condition:** 'Can you say what that would depend on?'
- **Explain:** Can you say *how* you would show that …?'

Keep the ball moving

Keep passing the ball to new speakers, and remember to pass not only to people with their hands up. Sometimes by simply allowing new contributions diversity happens naturally. The key to the success of this simple approach to facilitation is not to respond at all or, at the very most, with nothing more than a simple 'thank you'. *Echoing* (saying back, to the class, *exactly* what they said), or *eliciting* (asking them to say more) are also good default responses, if you must say something.

Remind them that they can put their hands up for one of two reasons: 1. to respond to the main question that has been asked; or 2. to respond to another speaker. The most common kinds of response are as follows:

- Agreement ('I agree …')
- Disagreement ('I disagree …')
- Synthesis ('I agree and disagree …')
- Add to ('I agree and …')
- Qualify ('I agree but/if …')
- Distinguish ('I agree but for a different reason …')
- Offer an alternative position ('What about …')
- Counter example ('But what if …')

If, after trying these two strategies, nothing much is happening, then try one or some of the following suggestions.

Response detectors

- 'Hands up if you have something to say about the last speaker's idea.' (The 'hands up if …' strategy.)
- 'Hands up if you want to answer the question and have something different to say to what's been said before.'
- 'Hands up if you have the same answer and have a different reason.'
- 'Put your thumbs up if you agree; your thumbs down if you disagree and put your thumbs sideways if you think something different to "agree" or "disagree".' (The 'thumb poll' strategy.)
- If the question is a closed question [e.g. 'Is it the same ship?']:
  - 'Hands up if you think "Yes, [e.g.] it is the same ship."' Take responses.
  - 'Hands up if you think "No, [e.g.] it's not the same ship."' Take responses.
  - 'Hands up if you think something different from just "yes" or "no".' Take responses.
- If someone says something that you suspect is or will be controversial: 'Is there anybody who would like to respond to the last speaker [or: insert student's name]?' (Note: Try to keep invitations like this open. If you always say, 'Does anyone disagree with that?' then you are only speaking to those that disagree, leaving out all those who agree or who think something other than agree or disagree.)

Right to reply

If someone challenges someone else or comments about someone else's idea, allow the person who has been challenged or commented on an opportunity to respond. Be transparent about why you are allowing one person more than one successive go, for example, 'It's only fair to let people defend themselves against a challenge.'

Talk-time

This is where the children turn to the person or people next to them to talk without the restrictions of a whole-class enquiry (see page xiii). Sometimes the class simply need to talk immediately, usually indicated by 'on-task disruption', i.e. talking to each other about something that has been said without regard for the rules, so use talk-time for this. Talk-time allows students to 'get something off their chest', especially if the idea they are all talking about is particularly controversial, but in addition to this it has the following benefits with regard to idea-diversity:

- Talk-time gives you a chance to go around and find out who is thinking what so that you have an idea where the ideas are, particularly the divergent ones, so that you can invite those ideas into the discussion when necessary.

- It allows those that don't put up their hands or those that 'haven't had a go yet' to say what's on their mind.
- It also allows the facilitator to find out what the less forthcoming students think.

Hands up/Hands down

To help with inclusion it is a good idea to identify who has spoken and who has not. I use the following strategy (for example): 'Hands up if you have something to say to the last speaker. Now, put your hands down if you've spoken already today.' If everyone puts their hands down, then say, 'OK, hands up if you have something to say to the last speaker. Now, put your hands down if you've spoken more than once already today.'

Tasking diversity

This is related to some of the 'response detectors' listed above, but is more systematic. Sometimes the best thing to do is to task the class to come up with as many different answers (or same answers/ different reasons) as they can. In order to gather the ideas together, you may even defer finding out their reasons (see 'Open up' earlier in Appendix 1) until later.

Providing contrasting examples

This can be a very effective way of bringing out problems and controversies. If I would like to begin an investigation into the nature of numbers with my class, I may begin by writing '2 2 2 2' on the board and then by asking: 'How many numbers are there?' This may be enough to get the class going but if not, then I will introduce some contrasting examples. I may write '0 0 0 0' and then ask the same question, or 'two II 二 ٢' (including, respectively, the English word, and the Roman, Chinese and Arabic characters), or 'two, to, too, "second number in the number line"', and ask the same question again. These contrasting examples are more likely to bring out controversies such as 'Is zero a number?' and 'Is a number different from the symbols that represent it?' that lie at the heart of the question 'What is a number?' See how the strategy of contrasting examples is made use of in 'The telekinetic teacher' on page 130.)

Imaginary disagreer

This strategy helps to create diversity by encouraging the class to actively seek alternative points of view. This is particularly helpful when unanimity threatens to stifle a good discussion. Ask the children to imagine someone who disagrees with them, then ask what they think they would say. The next step is to ask them what reason or reasons they think their 'imaginary disagreer' would give. This can be used with pairs, groups and also with the whole class. Sometimes the children will change their own minds because of what their imaginary disagreer said.

Random selection

From time to time it is important to pass the ball (or to select) those whose hands are not up, or whose hands are *never* up. Sometimes that really great idea that moves things along comes from someone who would have said nothing had they not been invited to do so.

Physicalise diversity

This involves having the students somehow represent what they think of the issue physically or spatially. By doing this the class all get a sense of the 'opinion landscape' concerning the question or issue. This can be done in a number of ways. I'll share two here but feel free to play around with these ideas:

- **Magnets:** Place a statement (either the task question in statement form, or something that's been said by another student) in the middle of the room, written on a piece of A4 paper. Then ask the entire class to stand up and place themselves at a relational distance to the statement, according to how far they agree or disagree with it. So, if they strongly agree they should stand on the statement, but if they strongly disagree they should stand by their chair (or by the wall, as some of the children I've done this with do). They can also place themselves anywhere in between the statement and their chair.

- **True/False:** Write 'True' on one piece of A4 paper and 'False' on another. Place these on the floor to form two categories. Have a statement (either the task question in statement form, or something that's been said by another student) written on a piece of paper. Ask students, one at a time, to respond to the statement by placing it in either of the two categories or in between, according to how far they agree or disagree with it. Always gently ask why someone has placed or moved the statement where they have.

Anonymity

In situations where what the students think may be affected by what others (peers or teachers) will think of what they say, anonymity can help to bring out the idea-diversity. The easiest way to do this is to have people write down what they think without writing their name on the paper. Explain to them that they are welcome to tell the others, *if they wish*, which idea is theirs but that they *do not have to*.

The different answer rule

Sometimes, the situation allows you to 'task' the children in a kind of 'game', where each child has to provide a different answer to *any other* child. So, when using this strategy, I might say, 'If someone else says the answer you were going to give, you have to try to think of a different answer!' For instance, as a response to a *thoughting* called 'Between My Ears' (see *Thoughtings*, page 12) I have the children list all the things they can think of that are between their ears. In order to encourage diversity, I use the 'different answer rule' strategy and it tends to mean that, as the activity goes on, they move away from the more obvious answers ('brain', 'ear wax', 'hair') to less obvious answers ('mind', 'information', 'thoughts').

Simultaneous responses

As you will find in 'Poles apart' on page 15, this is easier to do when the response is a one-word answer. If you are using the closed-question technique that I recommend (see above) then you should find many opportunities for one-word answers. In the case of 'Poles apart', all the children respond by *shouting out* (it's allowed in this session!), but you could also have them jot something down (it doesn't have to be any more than a simple 'yes' or 'no') on a small whiteboard and then have them lift the boards simultaneously to reveal their answers. This way, if there's only one person who thinks 'no', they are less likely to conform with the others than they are with a 'hands up' strategy.

Links

The If Machine: Section 1: How to Do Philosophical Enquiry in The Classroom pages 1–45; Facilitation and Speaker Management pages 19–28

The If Odyssey: Section 1: Classroom Techniques for *The If Odyssey*, pages 1–21

Once Upon an If: The Thinking Kit, pages 70¬–82

The Philosophy Shop: A quick guide to running a PhiE (Philosophical Enquiry), pages 10–12

Thoughtings: Appendix 1: How to Use a Thoughting (pages 191–193) and Appendix 2: Sample Lesson Plan (pages 195–198)

The Philosophy Foundation website: 'Blog' (free resource), 'Resources' (free resource), 'Become a member' (free resource) – www.philosophy-foundation.org

Innovate My School website: Peter Worley – http://www.innovatemyschool.com/industry-expert-articles/itemlist/user/1926-peterworley.html

APPENDIX 2:
THE LOST KEYS – THINKING ABOUT TEACHING INTERPRETATION

Texts – words and pictures

Picture books and stories are often used as stimuli for philosophy with children, and I think there are three main ways that they are used:

1. **Free-response:** This is where a story is told and the children respond either by formulating questions (P4C) or beginning a discussion and seeing if this leads to an emergent philosophical enquiry. There is no expectation about how they should interpret the story or about how well they should understand it. The level of the discussion is determined entirely by how they *do* understand it.

2. **Problems and dilemmas in narratives (e.g. the Odyssey/Arabian Nights):** This is when a story puts characters in particular situations where they are faced with a problem or dilemma. In the Odyssey there are many dilemmas and problems that beset Odysseus and his crew that can also be put to a reader or audience for philosophical consideration (for example, 'Should Odysseus tell the crew about Scylla, the monster hidden in the foliage?'). In order to make use of these scenarios for a philosophy enquiry it is important that the audience understand the plot and the dilemma. Here, there is a basic comprehension expectation from the children. (See *The If Odyssey*, *Once Upon an If*: 'Arabian Nights' and *The If Machine*: 'The Ceebie Stories')

3. **Stories as an engaging way to introduce a question/problem (e.g. 'Frog is a Hero' by Max Velthuijs):** this is where a story is told and then a question is asked (e.g. 'Is Frog a hero?') where the question 'What is a hero?' could have been asked without telling the story but where the story adds colour and context, offering the children something to engage *with* in order for the question to be put to them.

In *Once Upon an If* (page 16) I made a distinction between 'thinking with' and 'thinking about'. Now, however, I'd like to return to 'thinking about' stories. This means tackling something that many of the approaches to texts in philosophy with children do not: (critical) textual analysis. The PaRDeS method described below is related to The Concept Box method (see page 77 in *Once Upon an If*) and, like The Concept Box, it is designed to bring classes to tackle analogies, interpretation, symbolism and metaphor. Broadly speaking it is a hermeneutical – that is, to do with interpretation – approach to stories and picture books (see the introduction for more on hermeneutics). PaRDeS is so named after the acronym used in Jewish teaching to capture four levels of textual understanding. Although I have been inspired by the Jewish teaching approach and have borrowed the acronym, I have not adhered rigidly to the original understanding of these levels but have instead tried to make them more applicable to a contemporary British primary classroom context.

One benefit of this kind of approach is that it can 're-open' familiar books and stories. We have found, at The Philosophy Foundation, that philosophy is difficult to do using the traditional approaches (1–3 above) with well-worn books such as *The Gruffalo* and *Where the Wild Things Are*. This is because there are no surprises, so it's difficult to get the children to respond to a problem in a fresh way. But most of all, it is because the children have already been given many interpretations, either directly or indirectly, from reading these books through with adults – usually parents, grandparents and teachers. The PaRDeS method allows the children to enter – or re-enter – a critical relationship with these stories through a process of re-interpretation.

Here's how I've re-interpreted the levels of understanding from the Jewish PaRDeS teaching using the example of the Hodja story 'The lost keys'. First of all, here's my retelling of the story (which can also be used with classes if you wish; if you do so, then read the introduction to the Hodja on page 72 before telling/reading this story).

The Hodja and the Lost Keys

A friend of the Hodja found him on his knees under a street lamp near to where he lived.
 'What are you doing?' asked the Hodja's friend.
 'I am looking for my keys,' the Hodja explained.
 'Shall I help look for them?' his friend said.
 'That is very kind of you.'
His friend also went on to his knees, under the street lamp, and started to look for the keys too.

A little while later another of the Hodja's friends came by.
 'What are you two doing?' asked the other friend.
 'We are looking for the Hodja's keys,' the first friend explained.
 'Shall I help?'
 'That is very kind of you.'
Then, the second friend fell to his knees, under the street lamp, and started to look for the keys.

Eventually, the street under the street lamp was covered in friends of the Hodja, all on their hands and knees, helping him to look for his lost keys. Then one of them said, 'Hodja, are you sure you lost your keys here?'

'No, I didn't,' replied the Hodja, pointing, 'I lost them over there, by my front door, but it was far too dark over there to see.'

Levels of analysis

- **Literal level:** This is the basic comprehension level that asks a reader or audience to recall the content and order of events in the story. This may include *who* is in the story, *where* it happens, *when* it happens, *what* happens and *why* it happens. For example: 'In the story 'The Lost Keys' a man loses his keys in the dark by his door; he eventually has many of his friends help him look for them under a street lamp until it is revealed that he lost them somewhere else, by his door. The Hodja explains that he is looking for them under the street lamp for no other reason than it is lighter there!' One may also say what the story is *about*. Some children, when they say this, will simply mean *what happened* (see above) but others may use 'about' to refer to the themes of the story. For example, '"The Lost Keys" is a funny story about a foolish man who is looking for his keys in the wrong place when he knows it's the wrong place; it just doesn't suit him to look in the right place.' In this case, the child has moved towards the second level of understanding. As we see here, the transition will sometimes happen without any aid from the teacher; PaRDeS provides a systematic way of aiding the children *when needed*.

- **Moral level:** This is to do with what moral lesson or lessons are intended to be drawn from the story, or what virtues the text is suggesting we should possess. Examples of these can be found at the end of each of Aesop's Fables, literally spelled out. However, many stories will have an *implied* lesson for their reader/audience. For example: '"The Lost Keys" is teaching us that in order to find something one needs to look in the right place, not where it best suits the looker to look.' (See 'Mirrored' on page 142 for doing more with morals with your class).

- **Metaphorical level:** This is where the story functions analogously, sometimes symbolically, to represent or conceal a deeper meaning beyond a mere moral lesson. For example: '"The Lost Keys" may represent the following feature of the human condition: that the human being is only able to look where he/she can see; there are things the human being looks for that may lie outside of where he/she is able to look or see, such as God, objectivity, truth.'

- **Hidden level:** Sometimes a story can have a special significance for an individual that may or may not be something that others *do* or *should* see in the story. This would be a *subjective* interpretation of a text. And sometimes, there may be a legitimate interpretation of a story that has not yet been considered by the group, or, for that matter, by anyone! (What I will call an *alternative* interpretation.) These two ways of interpreting a text (subjective and alternative) afford the closest correspondence, short of oblique mysticism, that I have for the Jewish *sod* or 'hidden' level of understanding that may still have relevance and application in a primary classroom.

Applying PaRDeS (to be adapted as needed)

1. First of all tell, read or present the text (story, poem or other, such as wordless picture book).

2. For the **literal level** set the following task: 'Can you tell the class what happened in the text [insert title of story, poem or other – continue to insert as applicable where it says 'story' below] but in as few words as possible?' Here are some ways to help the class develop their thinking around the literal level that may also help them to move beyond it.

   - Challenge them: if someone does it in 30 words then say, 'Can anyone say what happened in the story in less than 30 words?'

   - If necessary, set stipulations: such as saying what happened in a) no more than three sentences, b) no more than one sentence (disallowing continuous '… and then … and then …'s) and c) no more than three words. (And what about one word? – See 'One-word epitaph' on page 3.)

   - You could ask a secondary question such as, 'Can you tell me what the story is about?'

   - You could ask a meta-question about the two questions: 'Is there a difference between saying what happened in the story and saying what the story is about?' (The former could be to do with events and the latter themes, for example.)

3. For the **moral level** ask the following task question: 'What, if anything, do you think we learn from the story?' Record their interpretations on the board.

4. For **critical engagement**, once their moral-lessons have been gathered, ask the following task questions, each designed to address a different aspect of interpretative analysis: critical engagement with a) their peers' interpretations and b) a moral of the text:

   - Do you agree with [insert other child's name who has offered an interpretation] that the story is about [insert their interpretation]? (This is for encouraging critical engagement with each other's interpretations.)

   - Do you agree that [insert lesson/moral, e.g. '… we should follow our dreams?']? (This is for inviting critical engagement with a moral reading.)

5. There is not much one can do to engineer bringing a reader or class to a **metaphorical level** of a text beyond a moral reading other than to take them through steps 1–4 and engage them in discussion. If the class is ready and able to reach this level, then given an opportunity (such as that which the PaRDeS method affords) they will do so, but if not, that's fine too. Regularly revisiting this method will allow them to do so when they are ready. The children can only go as far as they can go. However, PaRDeS provides an opportunity to optimise their ability to tackle interpretation. It won't necessarily get them to point Y, but it will give them the opportunity to practise getting to point Y. If they can't do it today, then perhaps they will tomorrow, or the day after that. In this way the PaRDeS method is diagnostic as well as – to some extent – instrumental. Another, possibly supplementary way to aid a class's transition into the metaphorical level is to use The Concept Box method (see page 77 in *Once Upon an If*).

The PaRDeS procedure is given a contextual explanation in the story 'The Pedlar of Swaffham' on page 94.

APPENDIX 3:
INTELLECTUAL VIRTUES

Here, I've identified some candidate, core intellectual virtues, excellences and/or competencies that it is hoped the children in your class will develop through doing philosophy that also have application in other subjects (you may also be able to develop an assessment tool for these competencies using this list):

1. To be **intellectually sensitive** – those taking part in philosophy will learn how to respond to others in an intellectually appropriate way (whether to be critical, logical, sequential, structural, semantic and so on).

2. To be **socially sensitive** – they will learn how to respond to others in a socially appropriate way (with respect, with confidence, tentatively, supportively, taking turns and so on) that is also intellectually sensitive (see 1).

3. To be **discerning** – they will learn to *recognise* and *distinguish between* different kinds of response, either to a question, problem, or peer.

4. To be **selective** – they will learn to select the appropriate response, either to a question, problem or peer that is both intellectually and socially sensitive (see 1 and 2).

5. To be **empathetic** – they will gain some insight about how their peers think and learn to approach problems from thinking with their peers, sometimes thinking on their behalf.

6. To be **critically collaborative** – they will practise how to appropriately *oppose* each other in the service of a collaborative effort to address controversies and problems. Importantly, it can be collaborative to be critical (see 1 and 2).

7. To be **coherent** – they will learn how to *structure* their thinking well, but also how to identify coherence and incoherence in themselves and others.

8. To be **articulate** – they will learn how to give clear *expression* to their thoughts so that others may understand them and therefore respond appropriately.

9. To be able to **abstract** – they will learn how to move from thinking *concretely* when necessary to thinking abstractly and more *generally* when necessary and to be able to apply abstract insights to the concrete.

10. To be able to **problematise** – to be able to recognise a genuine problem as a problem where one was not recognised before, either by oneself or others, or to recognise a problem or controversy introduced by a peer. I call this 'problem seeing'.

11. To be **re-evaluative** – how to judge when to re-evaluate (*revise* or *reject*) and when to defend their own and/or other's ideas.

12. To be **rational** – they will learn *how* to answer to the demands of reason and logic and how to recognise good and bad reasons. (*Critical thinking skills* enable one to exercise this virtue*)

13. To be **reasonable** – they will demonstrate a willingness to answer to the demands of reason.

14. To think **sequentially** – they will learn to approach problems in the right order according to rational, logical demands.

15. To be **Judicious** – they will practise *making judgments* with the aim of making good ones.

16. To be (judiciously) **resilient** – they will practise appropriate resilience in the face of other's opposition to their own ideas, and resilience to demonstrations made by others of shortcomings within their own positions and arguments.

17. To be (judiciously) **open-minded** – how to judge for themselves when to be open-minded and when to make a judgment on an issue or question.

18. To be (judiciously) **self-critical** – they will practise reflecting critically on the quality of their own reasoning and how to improve it.

19. To be **autonomous** – they will practise *thinking for themselves*, making judgments based on the quality of reasons and not on what others think when it would be wrong to do so.

20. To be **courageous** – they will be prepared to hold on to a belief if there are good reasons to do so, and they will be prepared to give up a belief if there are good reasons to do so, despite how difficult this may be and for whatever reason.

21. To be **comfortable with discomfort** – they will learn to appropriately challenge each other and accept that they may be appropriately challenged and that this may lead to feelings of discomfort, *and that this is acceptable*.

22. To **listen** well – they will practise how to listen *in order to understand* as best they can what it is their peers say so that they can properly engage, in a critically collaborative way (see 6), with their peers' ideas.

23. To be (judiciously) **supportive** – they will learn how how to offer *reasoned support* to a peer when it is judged appropriate to do so.

24. To be disposed to respond in the appropriate **psychological** way – they will learn how, once a problem has been recognised as a problem (see 10), to respond to *puzzlement* with *curiosity* and a *willingness to strategise how to approach the problem*. Not, perhaps, with *cynicism* and *helplessness*, for example.

25. To gain a **synoptic view** (an holistic overview) – they will learn to gain a sense of the conversation as a whole, and the various roles – their own included – played by group members during the conversation. This aspect is meta-cognitive and one of the more difficult intellectual virtues for young people to cultivate.

26. To have a **normative** aim – they will learn and cultivate a willingness to practise the intellectual virtues *as well as they are able* and to employ them appropriately (not misuse in the service of *sophistry*, for instance).

* See Warburton's A to Z of Thinking or Baggini's The Philosopher's Toolkit, for a fuller list of critical thinking skills mentioned at 12.

APPENDIX 4:
TALKING BOOKS – THINKING ABOUT DIALOGUING WITH BOOKS

In this section I would like to develop the idea of dialogues *in* stories to that of dialoguing *with* stories. One approach to working with stories, and particularly picture books, is to have the children generate their own questions in response to the story or picture book; another is to provide carefully chosen questions. Well, there's another: to have the children engage directly with the book itself as if they are conversing with it and the characters inside.

The words 'dialogue' and 'dialectic' refer to a two-way, critical, conversational relationship. In this section I will provide a few key ways in which a reader or audience can engage in this kind of relationship with stories and books, particularly picture books.

Tasks

Books and stories often set tasks for characters that can also become tasks for the class. For example, the story *Let's Do Nothing!* by Tony Facile has one of the characters set the task of doing nothing. As with the 'Doing philosophy' section (see page 68) the act of engaging the class in a specific task such as doing nothing itself becomes a stimulus to thought; something the audience can say, 'Hey, that's not possible!' to, among other things. The key to this approach is to set the class the task as soon as the task is set in the book. Stop reading it at that point and return to the story once the children have been engaged in the task (or thinking about it) for themselves.

Interesting examples

Often, when doing philosophy, one is trying to establish what something is around the question 'What is X?' (For example, 'What is courage?') One way to do this is by using an approach offered by Socrates two and a half thousand years ago: to test our answer against examples that seem, intuitively, to be right. Often, what are needed to really test a definition are examples that seem to be examples of whatever it is but that don't fit the definition. In other words, interesting and creative examples. Stories and picture books often provide such examples. For example, in the story *Knuffle Bunny* by Mo Willems, two contrasting examples of 'talking' are given: first, when the main character, Trixie, tries to communicate something while unable to use words, and second, right at the end, she says, 'Knuffle bunny'. These examples are enough to create controversy because they are special cases.

Morals and claims

Stories often have a moral, either explicit or implicit, for the readers or audience to critically engage with, such as this from *The Saddest King* by Chris Wormall: 'You should always be how you feel.' They also make claims about things, such as the many claims in the strange picture book *The Important Book* by Margaret Wise Brown, which include 'The important thing about an apple is that it is round.' All you need to do to engage a class with morals and claims is to ask the following task question:

Task question: ▶ **Do you agree with [insert claim made or moral]?**

(See 'The Lost Keys' for more on this and the PaRDeS method and 'Critical engagement' in Appendix 2.)

Questions

Books sometimes ask questions in the text. If you find a good question for an enquiry in the body of the text of a book, stop when the question is asked to run an enquiry. For instance, in the story *Frog and a Very Special Day* by Max Velthuijs, one of the characters asks, 'What does "Very Special" mean?'

Statements that can be 'questioned'

Even if a question is not asked, sometimes there is a statement made by a character, or in some other part of the text, that can easily be turned into a question. The title of the book *Frog is a Hero* by Max Velthuijs is one such statement; easily re-formulated into 'Is Frog a hero?' In the picture book *Shrek* by William Steig, the text says, 'There before him was the most stunningly ugly princess on the surface of the planet,' inviting the question: 'Is the princess beautiful?'

Definitions

In the story 'The Cookies' by Arnold Lobel, a definition is offered: 'Willpower is trying hard not to do something that you really want to do.' To use this, ask the class if they agree with the definition given.

Mistakes

Some books contain 'deliberate mistakes' for readers and audiences to spot. One such book is *Morris the Moose* by Bernard Wiseman, in which Morris's reasons for thinking that other animals are also moose are *fallacious* (see page xx). To use this, ask the class if they agree with the character that made the fallacious claim, in this case Morris.

Arguing with the book!

Following on from 'mistakes' – deliberate or otherwise – in stories, sometimes a book, such as Morris The Moose, will contain a disagreement between two or more characters. These books allow a facilitator to make use of the argumentative moves made by characters to critically engage with the children. Critically engaging with the children yourself is not advised, as there is clearly an unfair asymmetry between a teacher and small children. However, when the moves are in the book, then the facilitator simply represents the book or a character from the book at the appropriate time to encourage the children to dig deeper into the dialogue. For instance, a colleague of mine, Steven Hoggins, when working with very young children, reads through *The Cow That Laid an Egg* by Andy Cutbill and Russell Ayto and then asks the following questions: 'Is it a cow, a chicken or something else?' He uses the 'Definitely/Maybe' strategy (see page 153) to get them to be a little clearer. Then, if someone says 'It's a cow', he will turn to a certain page where one of the other cows in the story says that it's a chicken, in order to create a dialogue between the child and the (characters in the) book. As it happens the cow doesn't give a reason. If it did, then he could have asked the children to critically engage with the reason ('Do you agree with the cow?', see 'Critical engagement' in Appendix 2), but, as it doesn't he can enlist the children to think of a reason on the cow's behalf (a version of 'The imaginary disagreer' strategy, see page 122). If the children say 'It's a chicken', he turns to the last page where the cow holds whatever-it-is and calls it a cow, employing all the same strategies as before. *The Cow That Laid an Egg* omits any reasons for positions, but *Morris the Moose*, for instance, contains plenty of reasons to disagree/agree with. As you can see, both of these kinds of book can be used effectively in this dialogic, conversational way.

Links

See http://www.philosophy-foundation.org/resources/philosophy-foundation-publications/once-upon-an-if 'Thinking In Pictures' for more picture book suggestions.

APPENDIX 5:
THINKING ABOUT CREATING AND USING ENQUIRIES IN THE CURRICULUM

Landscapes and punctures

When planning your lessons, try to incorporate an element of enquiry into your planning. An enquiry can be anywhere from five minutes to sixty minutes and can be very useful for getting a sense – or 'view' – of your class's 'conceptual landscape': what they know about a topic, which concepts they have some – though a limited – grasp of, which they have *no* grasp of, and which they understand well. I would recommend running an enquiry for *diagnostic* purposes, *before* teaching a module, to 'see where they're at', and/or for *assessment* purposes, *after* you've taught the module to see how well they've understood and can apply what they've learned. Running an enquiry is like dipping a punctured inner-tube into a bucket of water; you can clearly see where the 'holes' are. Otherwise, you have to find them the hard way: by scrutinising every millimetre yourself. The relationship between facilitating an enquiry and teaching a lesson becomes clear and symbiotic when you use enquiries in this way: to find where the holes are, and to tell you what you need to teach, or go over again.

Preparation (before you work with the children)

1. Begin with your curriculum subject.

2. Concept-map (see page 88) the relevant concepts: main concept and sub-concepts.

3. Identify possible multiple meanings, distinctions and misconceptions.

4. X questions: Choose one or two central concepts that you will work with, and put these into a 'What is X?' structure to test them. Also use the negative version 'What is not X?' (children often find it easier to say what something is not than what it is), and see if you can say what's unique about X:

   • What is X? What is X not? What is special about X? (Conceptual aspect)

   • How do we know what X is? What do we know about X? (Knowledge aspect)

   • Why does X matter? (Value aspect)

5. Identify a controversy.

6. Think of a starting 'task question' (and accompanying 'nested questions'; questions that are conceptually linked to the start task question); a statement or task that will bring the children to see the controversy. It should be simple, it should contain key concept-words and it should lead to a controversy. You may do step 7 first and then do 6. (See 'Provoke' on page 6 for more ideas about how to start things off.)

7. Think of something (a scenario/situation, story, poem, puzzle etc.) that will help to bring out a controversy and that you can construct around the question you've formulated. Can you think of any contrasting examples?

8. Devise some extension activities.

Implementation

1. Run an enquiry (see page xiii). Remember to anchor the children back to the main question(s) and also remember to open up their answers. Remember also to use strategies for 'Facilitating idea-diversity' (see Appendix 1) rather than teach through the enquiry or have them 'guess what's in your head'.

2. At an appropriate time, and only if appropriate, explicitly ask the 'What is X?' question.

3. Augment this with a conceptual analysis exercise such as 'Break the circle' (see page 54).

   - Record responses.
   - Explore and (have the children) attempt to resolve any possible tensions.
   - Note the extent and limitations of the children's conceptual understanding. (Be on the look-out for your own limitations too!)
   - Note where teaching is needed.

You can try this with an example based on work I did with a teacher of seven- and eight-year-olds on incorporating enquiries into his weekly planning:

Preparation (before you work with the children)

1. Begin with your curriculum subject. For example:
   - 'Plants'

2. Concept-map (see page 88) the relevant concepts – main concept and sub-concepts:
   - e.g. 'cycle, life/growth, life, change, time'
   - Focus – 'growth'

3. Identify possible multiple meanings, distinctions and misconceptions.
   - e.g. 'build/grow', 'develop/grow', 'learn/grow', and so on

4. X questions:
   - What is growth? What is growth not? What is special about growth? (Conceptual aspect)
   - How do we know what growth is? What do we know about growth? (Knowledge aspect)
   - Why does growth matter? (Value aspect)

5. Identify a controversy.
   - e.g. something can get larger in some way but not be growing.

6. Think of a starting 'task question'.
   - Task question: Which of these things grow?
     - Nested questions:
       - What is growth?
       - Do none of them grow?
       - Do all of them grow?
       - Which do not grow? Why?

7. Think of something (a scenario/situation, story, poem, puzzle, etc.) that will help to bring out a controversy. For example (images on slides):
   - A: a plant
   - B: a building in construction
   - C: a child going up a ladder
   - D: a robot/android being upgraded (see 'The Ceebie Stories' in *The If Machine*)
   - E: a human being at different stages of life: a baby, an adult, an old person (where the 'old person' is clearly shorter than the 'adult')

8. Devise some extension activities. For example:

- Have the class do the 'from a seed to a tree' movement exercise, starting curled up in a ball and then slowly unfurling, standing up and spreading themselves out. **Task questions:** Did you just grow in the same way a tree does? Is there a difference between what you just did and what a tree does?

- Break the circle (see page 54)

Implementation

1. Run an enquiry (see page xiii).

2. At an appropriate time, and only if appropriate, explicitly ask the 'What is growth?' question.

3. Augment this with a conceptual analysis exercise such as 'Break the circle' (see page 54) on 'What is growth?':

- Record responses.

- Explore and attempt to resolve any possible tensions ('Growth is when something gets bigger'/ 'Learning is a kind of growing' – in this case the 'Carve it up!' strategy is called for, see page 30).

- Note the extent and limitations of the children's conceptual understanding and knowledge of the topic. ('You can't see them moving, so plants don't grow.')

- Note where teaching is needed. ('Plants don't know where the sun is because they haven't got any eyes.')

APPENDIX 6:
BE A PHILOSOPHER

Be a philosopher for UNESCO's World Philosophy Day (or any other day, for that matter!). If you like, put on a beret, but make sure you carry a small notebook and pencil wherever you go and spend the day thinking about one of the questions below. Try to stick to just one of the questions, and think about it deeply all day. To help you think, do the following:

- **Drink 'n' think:** Pour yourself a drink: a cup of tea, a cup of coffee or your favourite soft drink. Sit down somewhere comfortable and drink the drink slowly, thinking only about one chosen question for as long as it takes to finish your drink. Talking to yourself out loud is permitted.
- **Thought 'n' talk:** Find someone (a teacher – if they have time, a friend or family member) who is willing to spend five or more minutes discussing a chosen question with you. Read them the question and then discuss it together.
- **Write 'n' Reason:** Take a piece of paper (or your philosopher's notebook) and write your chosen question at the top of a clean page. Either simply free-write (just write what comes into your head) in answer to the question or, if you prefer, use the following structure.

Writing process

1. *Read* the question and have a think about it.
2. *Answer* the question. If it is an open question (not answerable with a 'yes' or 'no'), like 'How do you know what is true?', then answer by writing 'I know what is true because …' However, if the question is closed (can be answered with a 'yes' or 'no' to start with) such as 'Is there any reason to be good if you can get away with being bad?' then answer by writing 'Yes' or 'No'. It is often best at this point to go with your intuitions (your first thoughts on the issue) – it doesn't matter if you change your mind later.
3. *Justify* your answer (say why!): give any reasons you can think of for whatever you said at step 2 with a sentence beginning 'Because …' or 'I think this because …'
4. *Object*: try to think of what someone would say if they disagreed with you, or were to object to what you said at steps 2 and 3. Be as critical as you can with your first idea. Objections usually begin with words like 'But …' or 'However …' or 'On the other hand …'
5. *Reply*: Now think of what you should say in reply to the objection; in other words, how do you deal with it? You may need to do one of the following:
   - *Qualify*: 'If … then …'
   - *Clarify*: 'What I mean by X is …'
   - *Explain*: 'I will say more about X …'
   - *Revise*: 'Perhaps what I should have said is …'
   - *Reject*: 'I began thinking X but now I think not X because …' (or vice versa: 'I began by thinking not X but now I think X because …')
6. You may want or need to repeat steps 4 and 5 several more times before proceeding to 7.
7. *Consider*: Briefly think through the different points of view. Write a few lines for this part.
8. *Conclude*: Go back to the main question and state whether you still hold to what you wrote in answer to the question at 2 or whether you have changed your mind. A philosopher always looks for the best reasons.

Or, you could try your hand at writing a dialogue. To do this create two characters who disagree with each other. Give them appropriate names, such as 'Tom' and 'Jerry', or simply name them 'Phil' and 'Sophie', 'A' and 'B', 'Pro' and 'Contra', or 'For' and 'Against'.

Some big questions!

Here are some philosophical questions to get you started being a philosopher for the day:

- Is there any reason to be good if you can get away with being bad?
- Should you strive to live a good life?
- Is everything real?
- Are you the same person from one minute to the next?
- How do you know what is true?
- Can someone's opinion ever be wrong?
- Is the mind the same as the brain?
- Should life be fair?
- Is 'saying what you mean' the same as 'meaning what you say'?
- Are we in control of our lives?

This section can be photocopied and handed out to the students for them to read and do on UNESCO's World Philosophy Day (the third Thursday of November).

BIBLIOGRAPHY
NOTES

Foreword

1. March, J (1998). *Cassell's Dictionary of Classical Mythology*. London: Cassell & Company, p. 200.
2. Graves, R (1955). *The Greek Myths, Volume 1*. London: Penguin, p. 65.

Books

Baggini, J and Fosl, P (2010) *The Philosophers' Toolkit*. Chichester: Blackwell Publishing

Bartram, S (2004) *The Man on The Moon*. Gratham: The Templar Company Ltd.

Birch, D (2014) *Provocations*. Carmarthen: Crown House

Borges, J L (2000) *Labyrinths*. London: Penguin Modern Classics

Carroll, L (2010) *Alice's Adventures in Wonderland and Through The Looking Glass*. London: Bloomsbury Publishing Plc.

Cohen, M (2007) *101 Ethical Dilemmas*. Abingdon: Routledge

Cohen, M (2013) *101 Philosophy Problems*. Abingdon: Routledge

Cooper, J.M (1997) *Plato Complete Works*: 'Meno' (trans. By G.M.A Grube). Indiana: Hackett Publishing

Cutbill, A (2008) *The Cow That Laid an Egg*. London: Harper Collins

Day, A (2014) *The Numberverse*. Carmarthen: Crown House

Day, A and Worley, P (2012) *Thoughtings*. Carmarthen: Crown House

Dick, P. K (1999) *Beyond Lies The Wub: Volume One of The Collected Stories of Philip K. Dick*, London: Millennium

Donaldson, J (1999) *The Gruffalo*. London: Macmillan Children's Books

Fisher, R (1997) *Games For Thinking*. Winsford: Nash Pollack Publishing

Fucile, T (2012) *Let's Do Nothing*. Somerville: Candlewick Press

Gaut, B and M (2011) *Philosophy for Young Children*. Abingdon: Routledge

Gilbert, I (2007) *The Little Book of Thunks*. Carmarthen: Crown House

Graves, R (1955). *The Greek Myths, Volume 1*. London: Penguin

Hargreavers, R (2014) *Mr Good*. London: Egmont

King, S (2012) *On Writing*. London: Hodder Paperbacks

Law, S (2011) *The Complete Philosophy Files*. London: Orion Children's Books

Lewis, C and Smithka P, edited by (2011) *Doctor Who and Philosophy*. Chicago: Open Court

Lobel, A (2015) *Frog and Toad Together*. New York: Harper Collins

Lobel, A (2012) *Frog and Toad are Friends*. London: Harper Collins Children's Books

Longman (1991) *Dictionary of the English Language*. Essex: Longman Group

March, J (1998). *Cassell's Dictionary of Classical Mythology*. London: Cassell & Company

McCaughrean, G (2001) *100 World Myths and Legends*. London: Orion Children's Books

Sendak, M (2000) *Where the Wild Things Are*. London: Red Fox

Shapiro, D (2012) *Plato was Wrong! Footnotes on Doing Philosophy with Young People*. Plymouth: Rowman & Littlefield Education

Steig, W (2012) *Shrek*. London: Particular Books

Tzu, C (2006) *The Book of Chuang Tzu*, translated by Martin Palmer. London: Penguin Classics

Velthhuijs, M (2014) *Frog Is A Hero*. London: Anderson Press

Velthuijs, M (2015) *Frog and A Very Special Day*. London: Anderson Press

Warburton, N (2007) *Thinking from A to Z*. Abingdon: Routledge

Willems, M (2005) *Knuffle Bunny*. London: Walker Books Ltd.

Wise Brown, M (2007) *The Important Book*. New York: Harper Collins

Wiseman, B (1989) *Morris The Moose*. New York: Harper Collins

Worley, P (2014) *Once upon an If*. London: Bloomsbury Publishing Ltd.

Worley, P (2010) *The If Machine*. London: Bloomsbury Publishing Ltd.

Worley, P (2012) *The If Odyssey*. London: Bloomsbury Publishing Ltd.

Worley, P (2012) *The Philosophy Shop*. Carmarthen: Crown House

Wormell, C (2008) *The Saddest King*. London: Red Fox

Films

Monty Python and the Holy Grail. (1975) Feature film. Directed by Terry Gilliam and Terry Jones. [DVD]. UK: Columbia Tristar

The Time Machine. (1960) Directed by George Pal. [DVD]. USA: Warner Brothers

When Worlds Collide. (1951). Feature Film. Directed by Rudolph Maté. [DVD] USA: Paramount Home Entertainment

Online Resources

Institute De Practiques Philosophiques. (2015) Free Books. [Online]. Available from: http://www.pratiques-philosophiques.fr/livres-gratuits-2/?lang=en [Accessed: 29th September 2015]

The Philosophy Foundation. www.philosophy-foundation.org

Marvell, A (1650), The Garden. [Online]. Available from: http://www.poetryfoundation.org/poem/173948#about

University of Pittsburgh. (2013) The Man Who Became Rich Through a Dream. [Online] Available from: http://www.pitt.edu/~dash/type1645.html [Accessed 29th September 2015]

Here's a list of specific resources that you may find useful if you wish to explore facilitating discussions further:

Worley, P (2010) *The If Machine*: 'Section 1: How to do philosophical enquiry in the classroom', pp. 1-45.

Worley, P (2014) *Once Upon an If*: 'Storythinking', pp. 56-82 (especially 'Child-centred questioning', pp. 68-70)

Worley, P (2012) *The If Odyssey*: 'Logos: Teaching Strategies for Developing Reasoning' pp. 13-21

The Philosophy Foundation. (2012) Philosophy Now Radio Show. [Online]. Available from: http://goo.gl/pxlYMN [Accessed 29th September 2015]

The Philosophy Foundation. (2013) The Question X. [Download]. First published in Creative Teaching & Learning Volume 4.1. Available from: http://goo.gl/e5deJs

The Philosophy Foundation (2014) The Question X Revisited. [Download]. Available from: http://goo.gl/OGr0GS

Innovate My School (2011) Socratic Irony in The Classroom. [Online]. Available from: http://goo.gl/2y5vzz [Accessed 29th September 2015]

Innovate My School (2012) The Absent Teacher: Preparing Children for the Real World: http://goo.gl/tXyLk9 [Accessed 29th September 2015]

Worley, P (2012) *The Philosophy Shop*, pp. 1-12

Birch, D (2014) *Provocations*, pp. V-viii, 1-11

Weiss, M (Ed.) (2015) *The Socratic Handbook*: Worley essay, 'If it, Anchor it, Open it up: a closed, guided questioning technique'. Zurich: Lit Verlang

Kessels, J, Boers, E & Mostert, P (2009) *Free Space: Field Guide to Conversations*. Amsterdam: Boom

Magno, MD, Mostert, P & Van de Westhuizen, G (2010) *Learning Conversations: the Value of Interactive Learning*. Johannesburg: Heinemann